"In these pages I have heard the Lord speak again to me, re-minding me of what He has already said and taking me deeper."

—**Fr. John Paul Kuzma, O.F.M. Cap.**
Capuchin Formation Program, Borromeo Seminary, Cleveland

"Every once in a while, a book appears whose powerful simplic-ity can open our eyes to God's own vision of us. For those who struggle, as the author has, with a sense of worthlessness or self-rejection, this is that book."

—**Bishop John Michael Botean**
Bishop of Romanian Catholic Diocese in Canton

"This book is clearly a fruit of prayer. The reader is the recipient of the fruit of Mother's prayer, which leads us to the heart of the Father. It is there that we are fully seen, known, and loved."

—**Father Dave Pivonka, T.O.R.**
President of Franciscan University of Steubenville

"In *The Light of His Eyes*, Mother Iliana shares her gift with words to describe her own experiences of God's presence, mak-ing His presence visible to others—and she doesn't hold back! Her honesty about pain and sin, weakness and woundedness and feeling destroyed guides readers to the freedom of naked-ness before God. Mother Iliana helps us to break habits of holding on to a doubting heart, teaching us instead to open ourselves up to a truth that we might find too fearful to accept: that we are beloved children of God the Father, redeemed by the death and rising of His Son and able to call God 'Abba' in the Holy Spirit. This book is a reminder of how we need God's healing ointment throughout our lives. Being a child of God does not mean trying to earn our way into God's heart.

It means walking and growing in confidence and trust in Him. And Mother Iliana's words will help you do precisely that."

—Deacon Daniel Galadza
Professor of Byzantine and Eastern Christian Liturgy,
Pontifical Oriental Institute

"Mother Iliana's account of her journey from brokenness to healing will bring consolation to many who desire the true life that only God can provide. This sacramental transformation is accomplished for her as she becomes an 'insider' within the liturgy of the Church, as experienced in a Byzantine Catholic monastery. I hope that all who read this book will find in it an invitation to the deep personal conversion to which we all are called."

—**Fr. David Anderson**
Wyoming Catholic College

"In this little book, we sit at the feet of a young nun who has responded to our tears of anxiety and frustration by telling us a story she has received through her impressively vast immersion in the Holy Scriptures and her perception of God's voice in everyday experiences. The story is of the Father's patient and persistent proclamation of His love and affection for her. This vulnerably told story reveals an excruciatingly hard-won childlikeness, and it is truly a balm for a weary soul."

—**Fr. Michael O'Loughlin**
St. Mary's Byzantine Catholic Proto-Cathedral, Los Angeles,
and co-host of the podcast *What God Is Not*

"Welcome to the heart of Mother Iliana. Reading this spiritual testament of hers is like entering into the simplicity of Mother Teresa and sensing the fragrant devotion of St. Thérèse of

Lisieux. Through humble daily encounters and the sacramental vision to see through every one of these encounters to the Father's intimate love, Mother takes us into the heart of the spiritual life. We discover there that, truly and ultimately, we are His beloved sons and daughters, and every encounter of our lives, if we are open, can bring us to this truth. This is the lasting gift that this work of Mother's heart will give to anyone who reads it."

—Bill Donaghy
Senior lecturer and content specialist,
Theology of the Body Institute

"A grace-filled walk with a contemporary St. Thérèse, this book is for all those seeking security and rest in the Father's love. By way of witness, the Word, and childlike faith, Mother Iliana reveals the path to claiming the foundational grace of the Christian life: spiritual childhood."

—Sr. Mariae Agnus Dei, S.V.
Postulant director, Sisters of Life

"This is a simultaneously entertaining and deeply moving read. Mother Iliana explains deep, life-changing truths through vulnerable and simple personal stories. You cannot doubt our Lord's love for you after reading this! Thank you, Mother, for your beautiful, childlike heart, which shines forth on every page!"

—Sr. Thérèse Marie Iglesias
Franciscan Sisters, T.O.R. of Penance of the Sorrowful Mother

The Light of His Eyes

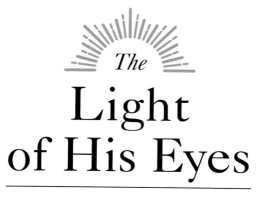

The

Light
of His Eyes

*Journeying from Self-Contempt
to the Father's Delight*

by Mother Iliana

SOPHIA INSTITUTE PRESS
Manchester, New Hampshire

Sophia Institute Press
Box 5284, Manchester, NH 03108
1-800-888-9344
www.SophiaInstitute.com

Sophia Institute Press is a registered trademark of Sophia Institute.

paperback ISBN 978-1-64413-872-4

ebook ISBN 978-1-64413-873-1

Library of Congress Control Number: 2023938900

2nd printing

Almost more than anything else in the Gospel
it proves that in God's eyes
being something comes before doing something.
He sets a little child among his apostles
as an example of what He loves.
He says that heaven is full of children.

—Caryll Houselander, *The Reed of God*

Contents

Icons

Foreword
by Fr. Boniface Hicks, O.S.B.

There are many questions that weigh heavy on every human heart, and they are reaching a fever pitch in our modern world as things seem to dissolve increasingly into meaninglessness: Who am I? Does my life matter? Is there really a greater purpose? Is there really a God? Can I really have a relationship with Him? These are profound philosophical questions that great thinkers have pondered for ages.

Mother Iliana ponders these questions in an unusual way. She does it in the manner of St. Thérèse of Lisieux.

The autobiography of St. Thérèse of Lisieux has touched the hearts of countless millions of people as she has become one of the most beloved saints in the history of the Church. What is it about her autobiography that has attracted the attention of such a wide variety of Christians? She speaks with a simple and straight-forward language. Her words flow naturally from the heart of a holy woman who has never lost the freshness of childhood. Her teaching is centered on Christ, flowing from the heart of the Church and saturated in sacred scripture. Her relationship with Jesus is so tender and so honest, and it makes her writing disarmingly vulnerable and personal. Her vulnerability opens the door for her thoughts to enter easily into the heart of the reader.

Consider an example from one of her best-known passages, quoted in the following paragraphs. Here she struggles openly, desiring more, and telling Jesus about it honestly. Her prayer is exposed for the reader to follow, tracing along the path from desires to thoughts to searching scripture and, ultimately, to receiving an answer through a graced discovery. And what she discovers is not only for her but also for us. That's the genius of the Little Doctor! She writes:

> No doubt, these three privileges sum up my true *vocation*: *Carmelite*, *Spouse*, *Mother*, and yet I feel within me other *vocations*. I feel the vocation of a WARRIOR, THE PRIEST, THE APOSTLE, THE DOCTOR, THE MARTYR. Finally, I feel the need and the desire of carrying out the most heroic deeds for *You, O Jesus*. . . .
>
> During my meditation, my desires caused me a veritable martyrdom, and I opened the Epistles of St. Paul to find some kind of answer. Chapters 12 and 13 of the First Epistle to the Corinthians fell under my eyes. I read there, the first of these chapters, that *all* cannot be apostles, prophets, doctors, etc., that the Church is composed of different members, and that the eye cannot be the hand at *one and the same time*. The answer was clear, but it did not fulfill my desires and gave me no peace. . . . Without becoming discouraged, I continued my reading, and this sentence consoled me: "Yet strive after THE BETTER GIFTS, and I point out to you a yet more excellent way."
>
> Then, in the excess of my delirious joy, I cried out: O Jesus, my Love . . . my vocation, at last I have found it. . . . MY VOCATION IS LOVE! Yes I have found my

place in the Church and it is You, O my God, who have given me this place; in the heart of the Church, my Mother, I shall be *Love*. Thus I shall be everything and thus my dream will be realized.... I am only a child, powerless and weak.... The heart of a child does not seek riches and glory.... She knows only one thing: to love You, O Jesus.[1]

St. Thérèse, in her childlike way, leads us straight into the heart of the Gospel. Her reflections are personal, simple, and profound. She captures the essence of the Faith and actually names the vocation of each one of us. Our vocation is love! She presents these truths in a way that is autobiographical, and her reflections demonstrate her holiness. And, at the same time, we feel she is one of us and that she speaks for each of us. There is nothing pretentious about her. Her struggles to understand herself and her faith are so accessible to us. She takes us along on a journey of discovery in which we can feel she expresses our own questions and then she helps us receive God's answers.

This beautiful little book that Mother Iliana has gifted to us touches my heart in similar ways. Mother Iliana has a way of expressing the most sublime truths in the simplest ways, and she does it all through the personal experience of her adventures in faith. She seems to skip through life with the buoyancy of a little child, and yet she makes her way through some of the most difficult and treacherous territories, including sin, shame, chronic illness, weakness, and poverty. She considers identity crises and personal woundedness.

[1] Saint Thérèse of Lisieux and Marc Foley, *Story of a Soul: Study Edition* (Washington, D.C: ICS Publications, 2005), 301–304.

Like St. Thérèse, her reflections are saturated with Sacred Scripture. She brings new light to both familiar and unfamiliar scripture passages through the simplicity of her own prayer and her hard-won personal insights. Like St. Thérèse, she touches the most tender places of our hearts where there can be so much shame, and yet she does it without judgment, and so she helps us with self-acceptance. She makes the love of God so tangible and so much easier to receive.

In her introduction, she says she is a painter not a writer; she says she is a nurse and not a theologian. In these pages, you will discover that she writes poetry with the paint brush of an artist, and she nurses little ones with her words that provide milk for all of us who are infants in Christ (cf. 1 Cor 3:2).

For example, consider this little gem of honesty and insight:

I went through a particular period in which I was deeply frustrated with myself because I thought I was praying poorly, frequently falling asleep and getting distracted. I apologized to Jesus and said, "I'm trying so hard to pray!" He responded, "Don't try. Just be. Be with Me just as you are." Tired, lonely, and poor—that is the place of encounter with God.

In her "painting" and "nursing" Mother Iliana's own unique personality comes out so beautifully, along with a picture of how she relates with God. On the one hand her way of relating—so saturated with Liturgy, Scripture, times of retreat and encounters in prayer—is inimitable. On the other hand, she teaches us about the way that God loves, about His faithfulness, and about how eagerly He desires to meet each one of us. She does not present her reflections so that we will try to imitate her way of relating with Him, but rather to give us confidence that God will draw close to us in the way that is best for us. In this way we discover the answers to the greatest questions as we learn them, like St. Thérèse and like Mother Iliana, from the Heart of Jesus.

And so I say to the reader: God knows you and with your permission He will develop His own way of relating with you personally. Mother Iliana will give you the courage to trust in that truth, if you let her take your hand and lead you into these pages with her. "And a little child shall lead them" (Isa. 11:6).

Introduction

What, my beloved, you realization of all desire, what, my beloved Lord, should I say to you while I am struck dumb with love? My heart is full of loving thoughts, if only my tongue could express them! What I experience is bottomless. What I love is endless; and therefore, what I want to say is wordless. "You are my King, you are my Lord, you are my Love, you are my Joy, you are my Hour of Gladness."

—Woodeene Koenig-Bricker, *Praying with the Saints*

Not too long ago, I began to understand what St. John meant when he said that if all the things Jesus said and did were written down, "the world itself could not contain the books that would be written" (John 21:25). Everything Jesus does is infinite; therefore, trying to describe all He does is also infinite. This might be the reason I find God so indescribable and have never had the desire to write a book about Him. It is also likely the reason I find myself easily overwhelmed when I undertake spiritual reading. The saints have written so much—where could I even begin?

As with all things in life, when we don't know what or how to do something, we turn to our Lord. He asked me to write this book in the moment that I had lost the desire for spiritual reading altogether. This is the great irony of this book and how the whole thing started. I had been on a little retreat, and while reading a fantastic book about prayer, I became frustrated. I threw the book down and exclaimed to the Lord, "I don't want to read *about* You anymore. I want *You!*" I realized that the most beautiful things I had ever learned about Him I had not read in books. No. Rather, they were things I knew because He had written them on my heart. And, in that same moment of realization, He wrote on my heart the content of this book.

I must admit—I was shaken. I immediately protested, as Moses had once protested: "But I'm a painter, not a writer! I paint precisely because I can't find the words to express what I feel. I'm a nurse, not a theologian. How could I ever write a book about the things of God?" My protests were futile, however, and I knew the futility of them even while I was protesting. But God did not require my ability. He asked only my consent. He was simply asking me to share with you the reason for my joy. The very heart of this joy comes from the knowledge, deep in my soul, that I am not just *a* child of God, but *His own* child, and that I delight His heart. His heart delights in me particularly.

To make sense of this for you, I am sharing a few stories about how I came to this understanding. I want to write this simply, as I would write a letter to a friend. I pray that "what has happened to me has really served to advance the gospel" (Phil. 1:12) by awakening within your own heart a deeper understanding of what it means to be His own child, to be the very light of His eyes.

Let the Children Come

In the Beginning

"God made someone really special when He made me!" Are you able to say those words and really mean them? I said them for the first time at the age of thirty-four, and I'll always remember it, because that moment changed my life. You see, deep down inside, I had always struggled with a feeling of worthlessness. I wasn't smart enough, I wasn't pretty enough, and I wasn't good enough. I didn't yet know and understand that I was the light of my heavenly Father's eyes.

I believe that each one of us, to a greater or lesser extent, feels that we are unlovable. But that voice in our heads that tries to bring us down from the inside out is really just Original Sin doing some of its finest work. After the Fall, we found ourselves naked, and since then we have been ashamed to be seen by others or by God in our nakedness. And yet a cry wells up in every human heart to be who God intended each of us to be—naked but unashamed. We desire the freedom of a small child who can run around his parents' yard with abandon, without a hint or trace of shame at his nakedness. We desire to run, just as we are, into the loving embrace of the Father. I am speaking, of course, of spiritual nakedness. We want to know that if, in the midst of our sin and misery, we expose the most vulnerable places of our hearts to God, we can remain confident that He still loves us—just as a child remains confident before a loving father.

Child of God

I had a spiritual father once who used to greet me in an unusual way. Rather than calling me by my name, whether he was walking toward me down a hallway or coming to sit next to me, he would greet me as "Child of God." I remember the first time he said this. I remember where I was sitting, what I was doing, and how I was feeling in that moment, because these words made such a deep impression on me. He was proclaiming a truth to my heart: I am God's child.

This is the most fundamental truth of our existence: we are God's children. St. John writes: "See what love the Father has given us, that we should be called children of God; and *so we are*" (1 John 3:1, emphasis added). There are no conditions added to this statement. We *are* God's children. St. Paul also states this plainly: "We are children of God" (Rom. 8:16). He loves us as a father loves his children, even if we think that we don't deserve to be loved. Caryll Houselander comments beautifully on what we know of God's love for children, and so what we know of His love for us, since every single one of us is His own child: "In God's eyes *being* something comes before *doing* something. He sets a little child among his apostles as an example of what He loves. He says that heaven is full of children."[2]

This struck me very deeply one night as I lay prostrate on the floor during Eucharistic Adoration. When it came time

---

[2] Caryll Houselander, *The Reed of God* (Notre Dame: Ave Maria Press, 2006), 32.

for the priest to bless the people, I stayed right where I was. I just rested. I did not need to know when it happened or how it happened. God was doing His work—whatever it was that needed to be done in my soul—without my needing to be aware of it. I was *being* instead of *doing*, *receiving* instead of *striving* to give, and the beauty of that receptivity overwhelmed me. It was a profound moment of freedom in my life, and it was so simple; in that moment, I was simply present before God as His child, knowing that I could do nothing to earn His love. He already loved me, before I did anything at all.

Loved in Our Littleness

I remember when I first discovered the freedom of being loved for who I was and not for what I did. During the Divine Liturgy, I noticed a small boy with his parents in the pew in front of me. He was very little, certainly younger than two years old. As the Eucharist was being consecrated, and as we attempted to ponder this great mystery, he stood in his pew, with his back to the altar, quietly playing with a little book. He was completely oblivious to what was happening around him. I looked at this child, and all I could see in that moment was God's great love for him. I knew in the depths of my heart that, although this child was ignorant of and oblivious to the great mysteries of God, he was inexpressibly loved by Him. He was loved simply because of the nature of who he was—a beloved child of God—not because of what he could do or what he knew. He was completely dependent on his parents for everything. He could not even receive the sacraments un-less his dad first scooped him into his arms and carried him to the altar. Yet, in spite of his complete helplessness, he was peaceful. He was able to be at rest because he knew his dad would take care of his needs, even when he did not know what his needs were.

Jesus says to His disciples, "Let the children come to me, and do not hinder them; for to such belongs the kingdom of heaven" (Matt. 19:14). There is something about these little ones that shows us who we are to the Father, what our relationship is with Him. We are all His little children. Are we not all, at the end of the day, ignorant of the great mysteries of God? They are, after all, beyond the comprehension of our human minds. Try as we might to understand it, are we not all somewhat oblivious to what is truly happening on the altar? And yet, in spite of our ignorance, He gazes with inexpressible love on those who have come to the altar to receive Him. At the Last Supper, Jesus calls His own who are there with Him "little children" (John 13:33). Can we open our ears well enough to hear Him saying this to us? For say it He does.

In the book of Wisdom, we hear, "How would anything have endured if you had not willed it? Or how would anything not called forth by you have been preserved? You spare all things, for they are yours, O Lord, you who love the living" (11:25–26, NRSVCE). Jesus says, "You did not choose me, but I chose you" (John 15:16, NRSVCE). And in Isaiah we hear, "I am the LORD, I have called you in righteousness, I have taken you by the hand" (42:6, NRSVCE). We would not be at this altar to receive Him if He had not first called to us. Like this little boy, we could not even receive the sacraments if our Father did not scoop us up and bring us to Himself.

But there is a difference between us and that little one. As we grow up, we become extremely self-sufficient and believe ourselves to be very much in control of our lives. We begin to forget that it is the Lord who has called us to Himself. We begin to forget that we are dependent on Him for everything and that, apart from God, we can do nothing (John 15:5). We become restless and anxious, and, just as we earn our wages through work, we begin to think that we have to earn God's love. We begin to be bound by the shame caused by our sin. We no longer rest in His unconditional love, and we forget how to lose ourselves in the security of His embrace. And so Jesus points to the little ones among us, showing us how we should be, as we once were—helpless and constantly in need of Him—resting in the knowledge that we are loved. We must remember that He takes care of our needs, even when we are not aware of what we need, for "your Father knows what you need before you ask him" (Matt. 6:8, NRSVCE). He shows us our worth, not by our strength or ability but by who we are: we are His children, made in His own image.

Children of Paradise

One day it struck me that, because there is no mention of Eve having any children prior to the Fall, there is no description in Genesis of a child's experience of the Garden of Eden. I began to wonder what it would have been like for a child to live in Paradise. I even imagined the way that children are sometimes portrayed in cartoons or fairy tales, in places where water or clouds or carpets are there to catch and carry them, or set them upright when they fall, resulting in peals of laughter and delight. What would the reality of the delight of Paradise have been from a child's perspective? Without being held back in caution by their parents from the countless dangers that typically surround us, they could have run and jumped and explored even the deep waters, a viper's nest or a lion's den, rocky formations, and so on. They would have been completely safe—only the tree of the knowledge of good and evil would need to be avoided, as a priest once lightheartedly pointed out to me. This freedom for almost anything, freedom from almost every fear, would truly be Paradise to a child's heart, for, much more so than adults, they are eager to run and explore their world. Children have an incredible capacity to delight.

I thought about how utterly joyful they would be, these children of Paradise, and even how joyful are any children who are now in Heaven with God. But then it struck me: Jesus says we must become like children to enter the Kingdom of Heaven (Matt. 18:3). "He says that heaven is full of children."[3] It is not *only* the children among us who will fully delight in the joys of Paradise, leaving us cynical and educated adults to find other ways to delight in God, *for it will only be the childlike who are there.* Our Lord further shows us that there is no use in us waiting until death to start being childlike when He teaches us to pray that it would be "on earth as it is in heaven" (Matt. 6:10). No, we must not wait. We must "turn and become," even now, "like children" (Matt. 18:3). It is only with such a conversion that we will begin to be filled with the joy of God, to delight in all that He does as we ought—as little children themselves do—and "like newborn babes, long for the pure spiritual milk, that by it [we] may grow up to salvation" (1 Pet. 2:2). This growth will be accomplished not in spiritual immaturity and childish "jealousy and strife" (1 Cor. 3:3), but with purity of heart in the humility of childlikeness—that is, the fruit of profound spiritual maturity. It is a mark of the saints to truly live as children of God, "on earth as it is in heaven" (Matt. 6:10).

[3] Houselander, *The Reed of God*, 32.

The Children Who Have Gone before Us

When I need a reminder of how other grown-ups have learned to embrace childlike simplicity and joy in their pursuit of Christ, I look no further than the saints. And how precious their relics are in such meditations! I simply treasure these relics of the saints. From praying at the tomb of St. Catherine of Siena to holding a tiny relic of St. John the Beloved in my hand, these encounters have always left me dumbfounded and overwhelmed with awe, love, and a longing for Heaven and holiness. These relics remind me that I am always surrounded by "so great a cloud of witnesses" (Heb. 12:1), and that I am not alone as I seek God's heart. Here are the ones who sought Him with their whole hearts, who have persevered through tremendous suffering and struggles, and here I am with them.

One day, as I was working on writing an icon, I had just finished the first phase of St. John the Beloved resting his head on the Lord's breast. The gold was adhered to the clay, and, like a child, I proudly went to show it to one of my sisters. I had never made an icon with so much gold before, and we both admired how brilliant it was in the light. I showed her the mistakes I had made and that I had accidentally left a fingerprint in the gold. There it would have to remain forever, because I did not know the technique for smoothing it out. "Well," my sister said, "now you are part of the icon."

The following morning, I caught a glimpse of that gold, and I thought of the fingerprint that could never be erased. I thought to myself that it was like a relic; if it had been the fingerprint of a saint, it would be treasured as a relic of that saint. Just imagine if we could see St. Luke's fingerprint in his icon of the Mother of God! We would rejoice and be in awe that we had seen it. We would want to take a picture and remember it always.

The Light of His Eyes

And then, all at once, I realized something, and I gasped. When God formed "my inward parts" and "knit me together in my mother's womb," "when I was being made in secret, intricately wrought in the depths of the earth" (Ps. 139:13, 15), did He not leave His fingerprint in me? Was I not created "in his own image" (Gen 1:27)? Is it any wonder that the Psalmist can cry out, "A wonder am I, and all your works are wonders" (Ps. 139:14, NJB)? If I can marvel over the fingerprint of a saint in a thin piece of gold, which in reality will eventually break down and be destroyed, how much more should I marvel that God Himself has imprinted His image in me? Through this revelation, I was awestruck by the great dignity of the human person, by the great beauty of His creation. I was in awe of this eternal soul that God gave to me when He formed me in the very likeness of Himself, when He made me to dwell in His presence forever. He has covered me with His fingerprints, created me, formed me, and has said, "Fear not, for I have redeemed you.... You are mine" (Isa. 43:1). "His banner over me [is] love" (Song of Sol. 2:4). As I seek Him with my whole heart, here He is with me. In a way, I myself am a relic, for my being holds the fingerprint of God, a fingerprint that can never be erased.

Am I Lovable?

I once went to a party and came to realize that I had spent most of the evening wondering what everyone else at the party was thinking of me. As I looked around, I noticed that I wasn't alone. I could tell by the looks of insecurity in people's faces that most of us waste a lot of energy wondering what everyone else thinks of us. Are we lovable? Are we good enough or funny enough? Do we make the cut? What is this invisible "cut" we need to make?

In the anxiety of this self-consciousness, we fail to see that we are—each one of us—the light of our Father's eyes. We fail to realize that He who made us delights in us, that He longs to lift us up from our misery, that He longs to raise us up to be truly and freely ourselves: the splendor of His creation. He longs to hold us, His own sons and daughters, to His heart—a heart that beats violently with love for each of us.

It is in pressing our ears to His chest and hearing each beat of His love that we will learn the truth of who we are in Him: we are His beloved children and the very light of His eyes. Knowing that truth will transform us, "from one degree of glory to another" (2 Cor. 3:18), in brighter and brighter glory, until we are so ablaze with the fire of that love that, when people see us, they will see His love. This is a book not just about being *a* child of God but about being *His own* child.

My Child

Father, here I am, and here You are with me.
    My sins masked my eyes
from Your steadfast Love.
    I thought it best to flee.

"My child," You called in dead of night,
    as tears streamed over my bed.
"When will I learn to do Your will?"
    I plead with all my might.

"You think it is by your own power that you glorify
    My name?
    But every day you make mistakes
And, seeing displeasure in people's looks,
    think I will be the same."

But then the lies are torn apart, and Truth comes as
    a balm.
    Your still, small voice says to the pain,
"I came for you who are so weak;
    now rest here in My palm."

Father, here I am, and here You are with me.
    No condemnation in this rest.
You've wiped away the shame, and now
    Your gaze of Love I see.

2

Our Father in Abandonment and Suffering

There Is a Difference

I remember one night that I went to a gathering for praise and Adoration. Confessions were available, but I hadn't planned on going; I was there to focus on personal prayer time. Suddenly, though, my attention was drawn to the words of one of the songs we were singing: "I'm no longer a slave to fear. I am a child of God." I soon realized that I *was*, in fact, a slave to fear, and I found myself running to the confessional. For my penance, the priest told me to ask the Father to help me receive His love as a child. As I sat down to pray, a wave of grace overcame me. I found myself praying this petition from my heart: "Father, give me the grace to receive Your love, not just as *a* child but as *Your* child."

Have you ever seen an adorable baby at the grocery store? I mean the kind of baby with irresistibly chubby cheeks and an easy smile, who seems ready to make friends with just about anyone. Most of us will instinctively smile or coo at such a baby as we pass by. We might even stop for a moment to admire the beauty of the child before we walk on to finish our shopping. We walk away because, even though he's a beautiful child, he's not *our* child. There is a difference between a stranger's child and your own. You cannot walk away from your own child, and, in most cases, even if the child walks away from his parent, that parent will be waiting for, searching for, and longing for the child's return. At least, that's the way it would be in an "ideal world," in ideal situations. We can all understand and appreciate this truth, for it is written on our hearts.

Broken Hearts

I grew up in a broken family. Coincidentally, this is something I have in common with each one of you. I know this, even though we have never met, because of Original Sin. No matter who we are, or where we come from, our parents and our siblings are sinners who, try as they might, have not loved us with a perfect love. It took me a very long time to accept this; it was too painful a subject for me to dwell on, and so I avoided looking at it closely enough to understand what was going on. As a result, I walked around carrying all these wounds that I did not even know existed. Why was it so painful for me to recognize that my family was broken?

The reason the pain of the broken family is so incredibly damaging to our psyche is precisely because it is the opposite of what we were made for. We were made to rest in the bosom of the perfect family, in the love of the Trinity. We were made for perfect love and perfect union. We were made to walk with God "in the garden in the cool of the day" (Gen. 3:8). The wounds we sustain from our broken upbringings penetrate deeply precisely because they pervert that which is originally made to be pure. Just as our ancestors once doubted the Father's provision and care for them in the garden, we also doubt the Father's care for us as we grow within the context of our imperfect families, for the devil has twisted and perverted the original beauty of the family.

As Tolstoy so succinctly put it in the opening line of *Anna Karenina*, all of our unhappy families are unhappy in their own way. When we were growing up, some of us had physically abusive dads while others had emotionally distant dads. Some of us were abandoned by our dads while others lost their dads through an untimely death. Every story is unique, and every story is painful. Each one of us is left feeling abandoned by our dads here on earth, and this leads us to believe that God has abandoned us too. Even those of us who had tender and loving dads have this wound because of one thing: sin. The trusting hearts we had as children—hearts that so naturally gave and received love—quickly become disillusioned by the sin that surrounds us. As we try to cope with our surroundings, these wounds lead to sins of our own. We develop the bad habit of doubting love, a habit rooted in fear that focuses on protecting our fragile hearts.

But the good news is that we all have something else in common too. Although we all come from broken human families, we have also all been adopted as God's children. In fact, we all have the same Father: God the Father. This makes each and every one of us brothers and sisters, something I did not always understand or appreciate. Instead, the brokenness that surrounded me in my immediate family would eventually lead me to despair, for I saw all around me families who seemed to "have it all together," a false image that led to heartbreak and jealousy. I could not accept that I was loved by God, no matter how many people told me, no matter how many times God showed Himself to me with the "signs and wonders" that surrounded me (Heb. 2:4). All of this despair came from a fundamental misunderstanding of who I am, namely, God's child. I was like an orphan who walked around in sorrow because she did not know that she had been adopted. Because I failed to open my arms to receive the love from God that He was offering to me—He, the God who is my true Father and the only one who would ever love me perfectly—I was starving for love. In such a state as I was in then, in such a state as I was in for many years, I might have starved to death looking for the love that I did in fact already have.

Not Abandoned

I remember once lying on the floor of my room, crying out to God, "There is no one who cares for my soul" (see Ps. 142:4). This was not strictly true, and even though I knew it, I was in too much pain to believe it. Yet, what is the truth? I hear the Lord whisper in my heart, "My father and my mother have forsaken me, but the LORD will take me up" (Ps. 27:10). The truth in the midst of all our brokenness is that, contrary to what we once thought, we have not been abandoned—the Father has taken us into Himself. Even as our bleeding hearts are crying out, "The LORD has forsaken me, my Lord has forgotten me" (Isa. 49:14), we hear the response of our true Father: "Can a woman forget her sucking child, that she should have no compassion on the son of her womb? Even these may forget, yet I will not forget you. Behold, I have graven you on the palms of my hands" (Isa. 49:15-16). When St. Paul tells us that we have received the "spirit of adoption" (Rom. 8:15, NAB), he is speaking this to a culture that knows the adopted son shared the same rights as the biological son.

This is incredible news! With God, we all live in that "ideal world" where abandonment is unthinkable, for we are all adopted as God's own children. It is very difficult for us to grasp this; it seems a foreign concept to us because we do live in a fallen world, but, as with all sin, "from the beginning it was not so" (Matt. 19:8). Although every story of our broken families is unique, all of us are the same in that, earthly abandoned children that we are, we all struggle to believe that God will not abandon us. This deep and penetrating wound can only be healed through grace. It takes great healing to believe that God never walks away from us. Even if we, His erring and wandering children, walk away and abandon Him, He, the faithful and ideal parent, is always waiting for, searching for, and longing for our return. And even in the midst of the greatest sufferings we might endure, God has not and will not abandon us.

Where Are You?

There was a period in my life in which I persistently asked Jesus in prayer why He had cried out the words "My God, my God, why have you forsaken me?" from the Cross (Matt. 27:46, NRSVCE). Though I had learned that, in that day and age, when a rabbi said the first line of a psalm, he was referring to the entire psalm, this more technical, historical answer was not enough for me. In my own struggles and pain, I really wanted to know why Jesus had said these specific words—words that would later be misunderstood by so many people. Of all the passages in the Old Testament that foreshadow Him and His suffering, why did He pick this particular one in this crucial moment? If He is God, why is He crying out to God? If He knows that God is His faithful helper, as the psalm later expresses, why did He even ask this question? With all of these questions in my own mind, I kept asking Him why He said those words. Finally, in a moment of darkness and stillness, I heard Him whisper an answer. In my heart, I heard His answer resound: "I cried out these words because it is the question cried in every human heart during every human suffering—'My God, where are You?'—and I answer, 'I am *here.*'" He is showing us that He Himself is the answer to the question, for He is in the very midst of our suffering. With this truth in mind, I can understand that, when I suffer, it is His suffering as much as it is mine. He has taken the pain of every suffering onto Himself.

When Jesus came to Mary and Martha after the death of their beloved brother Lazarus, both the sisters said to Jesus separately, "Lord, if you had been here, my brother would not have died" (for the full story, read John 11). Are these not the same words that are cried in every human heart during every human suffering? "God, if You had been here, my brother, my sister, my child, my spouse, my parent, my friend, my nation, my career, my body, my innocence, my dream would not have died! If You had only done *something*, I would not have this grief in my heart day and night" (Psalm 21 communicates all of these ideas). And yet Martha says something profound to Mary in the midst of this scene in John 11: "The Teacher is here and is calling for you" (John 11:28, NRSVCE). While I think, "If He *had only been* here," Martha reminds me that "the Teacher *is* here." Here in the midst of this sorrow and grief—here in the midst of my suffering—and He is calling for me.

Our Ability to Love Grows as We Choose to Accept Suffering

I remember being told once by a holy priest that all the problems in my broken family were my fault. These words sent me into utter despair. Later that night, when I lay in bed, I suddenly had the desire to pray for my family members. As I saw my dad in my mind's eye, my heart cried out, "Forgive

me. Forgive me for all the pain my sins have caused you." I
do not know, in fact, how culpable I am for the problems in
my family. Only God knows. But as I took the blame for it all
onto myself that night, I heard the Father say, "Now you are
more like Jesus. Though innocent, He took on the guilt of
all." This led to tremendous healing and grace. I found that
I now loved my family with a pure love, even those who had
done me wrong, because I was loving them with God's love
instead of my own.

In His love for us, God has created us free. We are free
to live in His love, to live according to His ways—and we are
free to abandon His ways and to choose evil. There is not a
single soul who is prevented from union with Him, except by
his own choice. It is we who walk away, not God; many have
walked away and chosen the perverse, inflicting the fruit of
their sin on innocent bystanders. Jesus tells us, "In the world
you have tribulation; but be of good cheer, I have overcome
the world" (John 16:33). He has overcome the world through
the power of His Cross.

The Father does not desire the suffering of His children;
rather, He remains with us in the midst of our suffering, calling us to unite our pain and anguish with that of His Son.
Even as Jesus is crying out, "My God, my God, why have you
forsaken me?" (Matt. 27:46, NRSVCE), He knows that He is
not abandoned by the Father, for He will also soon cry out,
"Father, into your hands I commend my spirit" (Luke 23:46,
NRSVCE). Jesus told His disciples before His Passion that
they would scatter and leave Him alone, but He says, "I am
not alone, for the Father is with me" (John 16:32, NRSVCE).
He casts Himself into the arms of the Father and saves the
whole world. What appeared to be abandonment instead

brought about salvation. What appeared to be abandonment instead allowed us to be adopted children of God. This is a great mystery. God does not want us to suffer, yet even suffering has lost its power under the blood of the Cross, where all wounds are healed and all creation is redeemed. "O death, where is your victory?" (1 Cor 15:55, NRSVCE).

Union of the Cross

When Jesus cries out, "My God, my God, why have you forsaken me?" from the Cross, He speaks in Aramaic: "*Eloi, Eloi, lama sabachthani?*" With the first two words sounding so much like the name of Elijah, some of the crowd mistakenly think that He is calling for Elijah to come and rescue Him (see Matt. 27:45–49). Since my monastic name is the feminine for Elijah, I was particularly struck by this misunderstanding as I prayed with this passage one day. The line "Wait, let us see whether Eli'jah will come to save him" (Matt. 27:49) seemed to jump off the page. As I read these words, I heard the Lord asking in the depths of my heart, "Well, Elijah, will you come and take Me down from the Cross?" My heart was pierced, and I was heartbroken, because of course I wanted to take Him off the Cross, but I knew I could not, because the salvation of the world depended on His "yes" to His Cross. And so, in my grief, I simply said, "No." And, at that very moment, He whispered to me, "Neither will I take you off yours, for it is the same Cross."

I think that we do not realize how much our suffering conforms us to Jesus. We do not see the tremendous value of suffering, and because it hurts, all we want is for it to go away. Yet St. Paul tells us that we are "always carrying in the body the death of Jesus, so that the life of Jesus may also be manifested in our bodies" (2 Cor. 4:10). Our suffering makes us more like Jesus, who, though innocent, took on the sufferings of us all. In our suffering, we are a visible Jesus in the world today.

A Crown of Thorns: Our Suffering in Union with Christ's

I once went for a follow-up neurology appointment for chronic migraine, and since the migraine was so severe, the neurologist recommended that I receive a nerve block that very day. That meant I'd be given a series of injections of bupivacaine (a numbing agent) into the nerves on my face and head. I had not expected any kind of treatment that day; my lack of expectation was really a blessing, as it meant I did not have a chance to get anxious about it. As my doctor was preparing the injections, I began to ponder what was happening. Having suffered from chronic migraine for a long time, I had often thought of the mystery of Jesus suffering with His crown of thorns and tried to unite my suffering with His. The tangible fact that numerous needles were about to be inserted into my head served to bring this image to the forefront of my prayer. Once my doctor began the injections, I had no doubt that He was allowing me to share in the mystery of His crowning.

When the needle is injected into a nerve, you immediately feel a very sharp pain—and the nerves on the face and head are particularly sensitive. The numbing agent burns as it is infused, but after a few seconds the pain goes away completely. As the neurologist injected nerve after nerve, it was the same pattern: terrible pain, followed by relief. I was immediately dumbfounded at what Jesus had gone through when He was crowned with thorns. How many thorns, I wondered, went through the nerves in His face and head? How in the world could He endure such pain, without any of the relief of the numbing agent to follow? He simply had this pain continuously. Then it suddenly struck me—these injections were teaching me how much I was loved! When I felt in my body what was in fact only the slightest glimmer of His suffering, it was impossible for me, in that moment, to think that I was not loved. No one would go through something like that unless they loved the person for whom they were undergoing such torment. Remember that it is the very night before He suffers that Jesus tells us, "Greater love has no man than this, that a man lay down his life for his friends. You are my friends" (John 15:13-14).

Our suffering, now joined with that of the Son, can mysteriously draw us more deeply into the knowledge of the Father's love and His desire to save us. The Cross of Jesus *is* the Father's love. This is the extreme He goes to in order to unite Himself with us for all eternity. Evil has now lost all its power to destroy, for now even death cannot separate us from the love of God (see Rom. 8:38-39). Now "we are more than conquerors through him who loved us" (Rom. 8:37), for "if God is for us, who is against us? He who did not spare his own Son but gave him up for us all, will he not also give us all things with him?" (Rom. 8:31-32). He has given us eternal life in Him. How prophetic are the words of the Psalmist, "The Lord is the stronghold of my life; of whom shall I be afraid? When evildoers assail me, uttering slanders against me, my adversaries and foes, they shall stumble and fall" (Ps. 27:1-2). There is no sin that cannot be redeemed, no wound that cannot be healed, no situation—no matter how painful—that cannot be transformed for His glory. Jesus tells us, in fact, that we are blessed, and that we can rejoice in the midst of our suffering. "Blessed are you when men revile you and persecute you and utter all kinds of evil against you falsely on my account. Rejoice and be glad, for your reward is great in heaven" (Matt. 5:11–12). Nothing is beyond repair. He makes "all things new" (Rev. 21:5).

St. John Chrysostom says:

> We do indeed die, but we do not continue in it; which is not to die at all. For the tyranny of death, and death indeed, is when he who dies is nevermore allowed to return to life. But when after dying is living, and that a better life, this is not death but sleep.[4]

Jesus, when He raises Jairus's daughter, says, "the girl is not dead but sleeping" (Matt. 9:24), and before raising Lazarus, He says, "Our friend Laz'arus has fallen asleep, but I go to awake him out of sleep" (John 11:11). "By Your word, O Word of God, Lazarus leaps up, restored to life."[5] And the word he hears is the Incarnate God calling him by his name. "Through Lazarus, Christ has already robbed you, O death. Where is your victory, O Hades? The weeping of Bethany is bequeathed to you. Let us raise branches of victory in honor of Christ."[6]

---

[4] *Catechism of the Ukrainian Catholic Church: Christ – Our Pascha*, 2nd ed. (Edmonton: Committee for the Catechism of the Ukrainian Greek Catholic Church, 2018), 79.

[5] "Lenten Triodion," Matins, Exaposteilarion for Lazarus Saturday, trans. from the original Greek by Fr. David Anderson, 2023.

[6] "Lenten Triodion," Matins, Exaposteilarion for Lazarus Saturday, trans. from the original Greek by Fr. David Anderson, 2023.

The Gift

My plans are set.
I stride steadily on the path,
sure of every step —
my journey cannot fail.

I do not expect
to be wounded on the way,
stripped by strangers,
left with nothing but pain.

Helpless, I cannot cry for aid,
yet those who see me flee,
recoiling from my wounds.
Now I am unclean.

I had thought I was strong,
but now, too weak to move,
I am carried by a donkey
and cannot even pay.

All night I groan
as a stranger bathes me.
Who is He that makes
my burden His own?

I wish I knew His name,
but, the next day, He's gone.

How will I find Him
to give Him His due?

As my wounds heal,
I think about His face,
and how He gently held me.
How did He know my name?

When I was young,
a victim of lawless men,
I saw the irretrievable
being taken from me.

Now I am old,
and see what was given:
an irreplaceable gift—
the Cross of Christ.

3

Infants with Royal Dignity

Child of the King

I remember one of my sisters telling me that I was Jesus. I could not understand this. I could accept that Jesus was *in* my heart, but I could not accept that I *was* Jesus. During one of my annual retreats, I was sitting outside under a tree, trying to read a psalm. As I went through it, I could tell that it was about Jesus, but I kept seeing the words as if they were about me. I would stop and try to straighten myself out, saying, "No, this is not about you. It's about Jesus." I would begin again, and again I would see myself in the text. This happened several times, until I heard these words in my heart, the same words that my sister had said to me: "You are Jesus." I asked Jesus to explain this to me. How could it be so? Then I heard in my heart, as if Mother Teresa was saying this to me directly, "Jesus, in the distressing disguise of the poor." Then I heard, "As you did it to one of the least of these my brethren, you did it to me" (see Matt. 25:31–46). And I was amazed at this new epiphany. I cried out, "I am poor, I am 'the least of these,' I am Jesus!" That evening I went for a walk. I did not walk where I had initially intended, because God redirected my steps, and so I met an elderly priest on the path. I said hello, and he looked at me and said, "You are Jesus. I can see it in your eyes." I nearly fell over. Then, as I walked away, he called out to me, "I know it's hard for you to believe that you are Jesus—even though you are, because I can see Him in you. Just try to imagine for a moment that you were. What would that be like?"

What would it be like to wake up one morning and realize that you are the child of the King, and the bride of the King's Son, and that He has given you everything? Have you ever sat with that and pondered what it really means? We all have one Father—God—and He has one Son—Jesus. On the day of His Crucifixion, Jesus, the Divine Bridegroom, consummated His marriage with His Bride the Church. We see this so clearly in the blood and water that pours from His side, as streams of "living water" (John 7:38). Through our Baptism, through water and the Spirit, we are transformed into God's child, welcomed into His very Body, the Church. He is the Bridegroom, and we are His Bride, and He has united us to Himself in a "one-flesh" union. We have become His own body, both suffering and rejoicing, in the world. We are children of the King, "and if children, then heirs, heirs of God and fellow heirs with Christ, provided we suffer with him in order that we may also be glorified with him" (Rom. 8:17). St. Paul writes to Timothy, "If we endure, we shall also reign with him" (2 Tim. 2:12). To be the child of the King means to inherit a Kingdom.

If you are finding this hard to accept, you are not alone, but I encourage you to not give up on the idea as a response to your initial and understandable lack of comprehension. Imagine for a moment, as I did, that this were true. Sit with it, and allow the Father to speak the truth to your heart in a way that you can receive it. Hear Him speak to you through the Scriptures and the *Catechism*, through the lens of your adoption as God's child, and you will begin to see more clearly. Ask Him, "Who am I?" St. Paul tells us that "just as the body is one and has many members, and all the members of the body, though many, are one body, so it is with Christ" (1 Cor. 12:12), and "it is no longer I who live, but Christ who lives in me" (Gal. 2:20). And again, "we are members one of another" (Eph. 4:25) and "members of the household of God" (Eph. 2:19). St. Peter tells us that "he has granted to us his precious and very great promises, that through these you may escape from the corruption that is in the world because of passion, and become partakers of the divine nature" (2 Pet. 1:4).

Clothing Jesus

There was a time, many years ago, when I was sick and hospitalized, unable to get out of bed, and the medical staff had to do everything for me. I was so completely helpless that I was able to accept their help graciously. I knew I needed them, and I surrendered. I can look back now and see how my attitude changed after I came home from the hospital and slowly regained more and more strength. An attitude of self-reliance began to seep back into me, and there were times when I really needed help, but I simply refused the offer of it when it came from my generous sisters. Instead of accepting help, I wanted to take care of myself. A few years later, while praying on retreat, I remembered a day when I had been sitting on my bed in my cell, unable to change my clothes. One of my sisters had offered to help, but I sent her away. It was humiliating to be so naked and needy. As I remembered this scene, I felt indignation rise within me, and before I knew what I was saying, I cried out to Jesus, "Why should I let her see me naked and clothe me?" I was stunned by these words, and I quietly wondered as

The Light of His Eyes

I realized that what I was asking was "Why should I be Jesus to her?" By sending my sister away, I was not allowing her to care for Jesus in the distressing disguise of the poor, for in our poverty and need, each one of us is Jesus.

Even if we do not yet fully understand, we begin to see more clearly that we are all children of one Father. We begin to see the great dignity of an adopted child of God. We begin to see that, through our Baptism, we share in the Divine Nature. Eventually, we will come to understand that we are called to love ourselves, our families, and all our brothers and sisters in Christ, with His own love in us. Mother Teresa wrote,

> Daily we pray, "Let them look up and see only Jesus," but how often [do] we look in and see only Jesus in us? Do we see Him in using our eyes, mind, and heart as His own? Are we so given to Him—that we find His eyes look through ours, His tongue speaking, His hands working, His feet walking, His heart loving? Do we really see only Jesus in us?[7]

A Man of Dust

St. Paul wrote to the Corinthians, "The first man was from the earth, a man of dust" (1 Cor. 15:47). Many years ago, I was returning home from an outing when, as I pulled the car into the garage, I suddenly noticed my hands on the steering wheel. As I looked at them, I spontaneously cried out, "My God, You are amazing! Look what You made out of dust!" Something reminded me of this moment more recently as I was praying in

---

[7] Mother Teresa, *Come Be My Light*, ed. Brian Kolodiejchuk, M.C. (New York: Doubleday, 2007), 231.

my icon corner in my cell. All of a sudden, like a flash of light, I thought, "But I'm allergic to dust. I'm very allergic to dust!" And I laughed a little at the comedy of it all; it was strange to me that I would be made from the same stuff to which I am allergic. This moment would become for me a wonderful analogy for understanding the absurdity of self-rejection. I've often thought that my autoimmune diseases were somewhat absurd. Why in the world would my body want to fight itself? And now, if I can take that thought one step further and into the spiritual life, how much more ridiculous is it for me to reject my very self—the amazing being that God made?

I was able to see that self-rejection is really a fruit of the Fall. In the garden, that "dust" was formed into the very image and likeness of God. In the garden, that "dust" walked with God. We were made to walk and talk with God in a lush, cool garden. Then came the Fall—I saw what I was made of, and I was ashamed. How could I, how could "dust," ever walk with God? And yet God had not wanted me to see the dust—He wanted me to see Him and to see that everything He made was "very good" (Gen. 1:31). He wanted to walk with me through Paradise, and He wanted me to delight in all that He had made—including myself. "And God saw *everything* that he had made, and behold, it was very good" (Gen. 1:31, emphasis added). Why do I think that He means everything but me? Instead of enabling me to persist in justifying such ungodly thoughts of self-rejection, this moment of revelation made it possible for me to instead cry out, "My God, You are amazing! Look what You made out of dust!" How could I reject what He made "very good"?

The next day, I read these words of St. Paul: "So we, though many, are one body in Christ, and individually members one of another" (Rom. 12:5). The words jumped off the page, as they are apt to do when the Holy Spirit opens our understanding and leads us to truth. If we are all one body in Christ, then my self-rejection is affecting a lot of people. If I reject myself, I am also rejecting my neighbor, who is one body with me in Christ. Just think of the person you love the most, perhaps your closest friend or relative. Can you imagine rejecting them? And yet, when you reject yourself, that is what you are doing, because you are one body with them in Christ. And if I am rejecting myself and my neighbor, then I am also rejecting Christ Jesus Himself, for we are His Body. This revelation made the words "Love your neighbor as yourself" (Mark 12:31) sound very new to my ears. Then I came across these words in Sirach: "My son, glorify yourself with humility, and ascribe to yourself honor according to your worth. Who will justify the man that sins against himself? And who will honor the man that dishonors his own life?" (10:28-29).

The Spirit of Adoption

I remember once visiting my very elderly grandmother. She had severe dementia; even though I was sitting next to her, she would forget that I was there. To help her remember, I finally sat down on the ground in front of her. She gazed at me for a long time, and I gazed back at her. Finally, she said, "You know, you look a lot like my children!" About a year later, I found myself gazing at her once more as she lay in a hospital bed. I was not quite sure if she knew who I was, but as she returned my gaze, she finally said with great joy, "You look a lot like me!"

Just as my grandmother did in those two moments, when the Father looks at us, He sees His Son, and He sees Himself.

Because Jesus took on our human nature, human nature is now an inseparable part of the love of the Trinity. We are now a part of God, and it is impossible to separate ourselves from His love. It is an incredible mystery that I cannot fully understand, but I can believe it because of "faith in the Son of God, who loved me and gave himself for me" (Gal. 2:20).

As I began to understand this familial identity and reflection that God has given us through Jesus, I was thinking one day on the words of Jesus to His disciples at the Last Supper. He told them, "The Father himself loves you, because you have loved me" (John 16:27). I did not understand what I was reading. Are we loved by the Father simply for loving Jesus? I closed my eyes and, as I prayed, I saw a woman walking. I asked her what she was doing and where she was going. She pointed and said, "This is where He was condemned. I walk where He walks." I saw Jesus condemned. I saw Him in the garden in agony. I saw Him as He carried His Cross. I saw Him on the Cross. I heard again, "I walk where He walks." He walked on the way of temptation, and He overcame it. He walked on the way of fear, and He overcame it. He walked on the way of pain, humiliation, mockery, and death, and He overcame them all. "I walk where He walks." I must be condemned with Him. I must carry my cross with Him — my crosses are my portion of His same Cross. But also, when my crosses are overcome, I am able to share in His joy with Him.

I asked myself, "Why did He overcome?" The answer came right away, though it would take another year of prayer for me to even begin to understand it. He overcame because of His union with the will of the Father. He overcame because He knew that He was loved. He overcame because He knew *who* He was to the Father. He knew He was the "beloved Son" (Matt. 3:17).

The Light of His Eyes

Think about it. If we are loved simply for loving the Son, how loved is that Son? This is a love beyond all our imagining, and we, as adopted children of the Father, now share in this very sonship. In this sharing, I see that if I am loved because I love the Son, the Son is also loved because He loves me. There is no disunity in this love; there is simply a continuous outpouring of love from the Father to the Son, from the Father to me, and I, by adoption, share in the sonship of the Son. When the Father sees me, He sees two things: He sees the Son, and He sees who the Son loves. Jesus says, "He who loves me will be loved by my Father" (John 14:21). I have become the Son, and I am loved by the Son, and the Son in me is loved by the Father. If all this sounds confusing, it is only because trying to describe with words something infinite and alive is quite impossible — just as it is impossible for the Father to not love you, because He Himself *is* love (see 1 John 4:8). Love itself is loving you, and this is a love that cannot be quenched (see Song of Sol. 8:7). This is what it means to be an adopted child of God.

I continued to search the Gospel of John for some confirmation of these reflections, and I read, "As the Father has loved *me*, so have I loved *you*" (15:9, emphasis added). Can it be, I wondered, that God loves us as much as He loves Himself? And why should He not? After all, He taught us to love our neighbor as ourselves (see Mark 12:31 and Lev. 19:18). Why should He not love His own children as Himself? And Christ's presence in us confirms this, "for God so loved the world that he gave his only Son, that whoever believes in him should not perish but have eternal life" (John 3:16). We can hear His love in His words throughout Scripture, as when He calls to His people, "You are precious in my eyes, and honored, and I love you" (Isa. 43:4).

Through the Lens of Baby Feet

During one of my annual retreats, my director once invited me to a Baptism. I hesitated to attend at first, since I did not know the family. I did not want to intrude on their special day. I was not yet able to see that even though I had never met them, they were, in Christ, my own family. The baby's name was Josephine. She was a month old, and breathtakingly beautiful. I wept during the Baptism because I could see God's will for her so clearly. She was being brought into God's family, being adopted as His own daughter. She was called to be a saint. Her whole life was for God's glory. In fact, she was holy. As her mom held her, her two little legs dangled off the edge of her mother's arm. Throughout the rest of my retreat, I kept seeing her little feet in my mind—tiny, soft, and precious. I saw her innocence, newly immersed in baptismal grace.

Later, as I was praying with a passage from the prophet Isaiah, I came across these words: "You shall be a crown of beauty in the hand of the LORD, and a royal diadem in the hand of your God.... You shall be called My delight is in her" (Isa. 62:3–4). I saw a little child, simply held in His arms. I saw the souls of the saints in His hands—more precious than jewels—and His delight in them. Then I saw the image of Josephine, so tiny and precious, and her little feet draped over her mother's arm. I heard the words "All glorious the king's daughter enters" (see Ps. 45:13), and I saw how Josephine was brought into the house of God, resplendent with baptismal grace. I understood that she herself was the house of God now, because the King of glory had made His home within her (see John 14:23, Luke 17:21, Rev. 3:20). I began to realize that I was as small to the Father as Josephine, for I too was the King's daughter. When we reach adulthood, we begin to suffer from an illusion that we are very big; in fact, we are just infants in His eyes.

During Matins the following day, we prayed, "O Lord, *I love* the house in which you dwell, and the place where your glory abides" (Ps. 26:8, NRSVCE, emphasis added), and an arrow of truth illumined my understanding. I knew that I too was the house of God, the place where His glory abides, and that He was asking me to love myself. I saw baby Josephine again, and the love He had for her: Josephine, the house of God; Josephine, the temple of the Holy Spirit (see 1 Pet. 2:5 and 1 Cor. 6:19). He loves her, and He was asking me to not hate what He loves, what He finds precious. How could I hate what He loves? In that moment, I saw all the wounds of self-hatred from my past for what they were—complete and utter lies.

Then I remembered, when her parents came to greet me and show her off, how tenderly she had been handed to me. It struck me that, as we get older, we lose that tenderness. We begin to get rough with each other. Our defenses are built up, we fear getting hurt, and we develop tougher hearts. But each of us is, in reality, as delicate as little Josephine, and God calls us to care for one another as delicately as we would care for a newborn baby. Many memories from my time working in the neonatal intensive care unit resurfaced; they drove home the realization that every single one of us is not just a little baby but a *wounded* little baby—so in need of gentle and compassionate care.

A few days after this Baptism, I was praying the Rosary with another nun. When we came to the Mystery of the Presentation of Our Lord in the Temple, I saw Josephine's feet again, and I heard the Lord whisper, "They were My feet." Later that day, I was praying with the passage in the Gospel of Luke that tells us of Jesus' visit to Martha and Mary (see 10:38-42). I noticed that Jesus had entered the home of Martha and Mary, as He has entered into me, who is the house of God. Martha was distracted, but Mary simply sat at His feet and listened. Suddenly, He reminded me of Josephine's feet and whispered again, "They were My feet." I realized that, in being with Josephine, I had been resting at Jesus' feet, the one thing that was needful for me to do. She was Jesus. You are Jesus. He was calling me to hold you as tenderly in my hands as I held Josephine—as tenderly as He Himself is holding you, His own little one.

And so it continued. Every day of that retreat, I would see Josephine's feet in my prayers. During midday prayers, as I was reminded of her feet again, I realized that they belonged to someone totally naked and helpless. She could not sit up to look at something, she could not grab any food with her hands if she felt hungry, she could not cover herself if she felt cold, and she could not toilet herself. She was naked, helpless, and dependent, and yet God Himself entered into this state; He became an infant, and He asks us to do the same. He asks us to be like little infants in the arms of the Father—the Father who sees His Son in us, the Father who loves us without limit.

Sacred Temple

Just as we start to get rough with each other as we get older, we also start to get rough with ourselves. It was so obvious to me that newly baptized and innocent little Josephine was now the house of God, the temple of the Holy Spirit. Why is it so hard to believe that I am too? Why have I spent decades and decades of energy battling feelings of shame and self-rejection, when in fact I am just as innocent and little as Josephine every time I walk out of the confessional? When the Father speaks to His people through the prophet Jeremiah, assuring that

He "remember[s] their sin no more" (Jer. 31:34), why do we not believe Him?

I once asked the Father in prayer if He wanted to speak a word to me. The only word I heard in my heart was "temple." After praying with that word for a while, and considering what it means to be a temple of the Holy Spirit, I heard these words in my heart: "Do not profane what is holy. Cherish it." As I pondered these words, I realized that He was speaking about me. When I fall into the traps of self-rejection, it is a profanation of the temple of God. I would not dream of profaning the temple of God, or so I thought, yet every time I reject myself, that is exactly what I am doing. God was asking me to cherish what He cherishes. He was asking me to delight in what He delights in.

When was the last time you allowed the Father to delight in you as He delights in His own beloved Son? Do you think He loves the Son more than He loves you? That simply is not possible, for God *is* love. He cannot love one more than another. He simply loves. This is the truth that the devil has tried to squelch in us from the very beginning, the truth above all other truths. The devil torments us with these doubts because he knows that if God's children truly knew and believed how perfectly they are loved, they would cast themselves into this love with all their hearts, and the face of the earth would be transformed. You are loved by the Father as Jesus is loved by the Father. The only question is—and this is vitally important—*will you receive this love?*

Receiving the Kingdom

During Matins one morning, I remembered a scene from the movie *Jesus of Nazareth*. I grew up watching it frequently, and the scene was vivid in my mind: Salome dancing before King Herod. "What a strange distraction," I thought, as we were not singing about John the Baptist, or Herod, or Salome, or anything else that might remind me of this scene. Then I came to my cell to pray. I began to read where I had left off in my daily New Testament reading, and halfway through the chapter in Mark, I came across the scene of Salome dancing before King Herod. I was so astonished that this was the very thing I had been thinking about—and was even distracted by—just a few moments earlier, so I made sure to pay close attention to this passage. I was sure God was trying to show me something about Himself.

The words that struck me were the rash words of King Herod to Salome after her dance: "Whatever you ask me, I will give you, even half of my kingdom" (Mark 6:23). Immediately this thought came to my mind: "Whereas the children of darkness receive only half of a fleeting kingdom, the children of God receive a whole and eternal Kingdom."

All the riches of this world are passing away. All kingdoms of this earth will wither away like grass. All the most powerful people—the ones with the greatest wealth or control or learning—will fade like a passing wind. To receive half of their power, you would have to earn your way, even dance your way to the top, so to speak. But, for the children of God, it is so different. He paid the price of our inheritance Himself, with His own blood on the Cross. We do not have to earn our inheritance—we are His children and heirs. St. Paul clearly describes what it means to be a child of God, saying,

> For you did not receive the spirit of slavery to fall back into fear, but you have received the spirit of sonship.

The Light of His Eyes

> When we cry "Abba! Father!" it is the Spirit himself
> bearing witness with our spirit that we are children
> of God, and if children, then heirs, heirs of God and
> fellow heirs with Christ. (Rom. 8:15–17)

This reminds me of a homily I once heard about the rich
young man (see Mark 10:17–22). He asks Jesus what he must
do to *inherit* eternal life. The priest pointed out that this was
a strange question, indeed, saying, "You don't have to *do* anything to inherit. You inherit because of who you *are*." Even the
children of this world receive inheritances from their parents,
yet even these are entirely fleeting.

This thought, in turn, reminds me of the statue in King
Nebuchadnezzar's dream (see Dan. 2:17–45). All the kingdoms
of the earth, represented as gold, silver, bronze, iron, and
clay, are utterly destroyed by the stone "cut out by no human
hand" (Dan. 2:34). This stone is Christ, and His Kingdom
"shall never be destroyed" (Dan. 2:44). I am also reminded of
Moses' exhortation to the Chosen People: "I have set before
you life and death, blessing and curse; therefore choose life,
that you and your descendants may live" (Deut. 30:19). And
again, Joshua exhorts, "Choose this day whom you will serve"
(Josh. 24:15). The question is, which kingdom will we choose?
Which kingdom will we *receive* as our inheritance? Will we
embrace half of a fleeting kingdom, which looks so comfort-
able and appealing now, or will we live as people who hope
and await the whole and eternal Kingdom of God?

Our Identity under Attack

The answers to these questions should be "no-brainers," but
the problem is that we don't actually know who we are. Even

if some part of our brain knows it, we struggle tremendously to really believe it and to live out that belief. Do we live as children of God, with all that entails? Do we live as beloved, cherished, precious heirs to an eternal Kingdom?

It's a problem of a universal identity crisis. Once, when I was on a retreat, I simply sat on the floor and cried out to Jesus, "Son of David, have mercy on me!" He turned and said, "What do you want me to do for you?" (see Luke 18:35-43). I responded spontaneously, "I am covered with wounds. People have mocked me, and I don't know who I am anymore. I want to be healed. I want to be wholly who you made me to be!" He lifted His hands to me and said, "I have wounds too. Look at what people did to Me. But I know who I am to the Father. I know I am His beloved Son." Each one of us needs to hear the Father say to us, "This is My beloved Son, in whom I am well pleased," for when the Father sees each one of us, He sees Jesus—He sees His beloved Son. And this, our true identity, is attacked more than anything else. Satan even tries to tempt Jesus Himself to doubt who He is: "If you are the Son of God, command these stones to become loaves of bread," and "If you are the Son of God, throw yourself down" from the pinnacle (see Matt. 4:1-11). If Satan does that to Jesus, whom he cannot possibly succeed in fooling, how much more is he doing that to each of us, whom he knows to be so weak, vulnerable, and fearful?

The Temple of the Living God

I sway in prayer, stricken with grief,
    beholding the ruins
    that the glory cloud abandoned long ago.

Come, Lord, to the place of Your rest,
    You and Your holy Ark!
    God, my God, why have You abandoned me?

I am small, easily overlooked, poor and needy,
    yet the Lord thinks of me.

Watching, observing the cold rocks,
    I become still.

In the silence, I hear my name.
    He must stay in my house? Hurry?
    He is coming today? He is coming now?

My heart skips—my house?
    My house lies in ruins.

A glimmer—light pierces the darkness.
    The Kingdom of God is within me—
    I am the house.

I look down to see with the eyes of my soul—
    the glory cloud is here,
    here in the temple of my body.

4

Anointing the Wound

The Prime Temptation

Retreats can be a truly powerful time for conversion, healing, and attaining a deeper understanding of God's love for us. If you are struggling to receive the Father's love, I would recommend taking time to be alone with Him. Know that He is with you always (Matt. 28:20), but set aside time just for prayer. Cry out to Him, tell Him everything that hurts, and write down what you hear. You will find that these graces will grow within you over years, and over your whole life. What He showed me on retreat years ago, for example—that day I sat on the floor and cried out for Him to have pity on me—is opening a new level of receptivity and understanding within me today as I write this book.

Until today, I had not remembered making that prayer, nor had I remembered His response as I related it in the previous chapter. Yet, at this moment, I can see that even now, years later, He is deepening my understanding of this very same truth. I find myself filled with wonder at the great patience and steadfast love of the Father, who sends us the Holy Spirit to guide us "into all the truth" (John 16:13). This understanding does not come all at once—it is too big for that. It comes over a lifetime.

What is very striking to me in this encounter is Jesus' emphasis on knowing who He is: the beloved Son. When Jesus rises from the baptismal waters of the Jordan, the voice of the Father is heard saying, "This is my beloved Son, with whom I am well pleased" (Matt. 3:17). This voice did not come just to catechize those at the Jordan that day; it came also that the Son might hear it. Immediately after this, Jesus enters the wilderness and "Satan tempts him three times, seeking to compromise his *filial attitude* toward God" (CCC 538, emphasis added). Just as that is the primary temptation in the wilderness, so too is it the primary temptation in our lives—a temptation to despair of our sonship with the Father. The wound in our lives that most needs to be touched by God's grace and that most needs to be healed is the lie that we are not beloved of the Father.

Balm for the Wound

One day, during my prayer time, I became distracted with the sudden realization that a little cut on my finger was hurting. I looked down and noticed that it had dried out, and I just chuckled and thought to myself, "Wounds sure need a lot of moisture!" I had not intended this remark to turn into a spiritual reflection, but as everything that is united to God becomes infinite, this little comment became a source of infinite grace within my soul. I began to see God's hand in this little remark.

I had a lot of physical wounds around that time. It was somewhat burdensome; every evening, they would have to be cleansed, and because these areas of skin breakdown were on my back, where I could not reach them, one of my sisters would have to come and put ointment and bandages on them. This routine lasted for about two and a half weeks, and just as with the cut on my hand, I soon noticed that the broken skin on my back needed a lot of moisture. If I left the bandages off any one of these wounds for any length of time, it would begin to dry out, start cracking, and would cause a lot of pain.

Suddenly, I could see that the moisture from these ointments, received from the generous and caring hands of my sisters, was analogous to the mercy of God. One drop of ointment was enough to stop the pain of these physical wounds, just as one drop of His mercy runs down into our spiritual wounds to take the pain away. I also noticed, however, that one drop was not actually enough for any lasting relief; to *heal* each wound, I had to accept that it would take a lot of time and many repeated drops of ointment. This image reminded me of what happens in confession: repeated drops of ointment, given frequently for the rest of our lives, until the day we are truly healed and beholding Him face-to-face.

I could also see that He wants to share in all of it. Nothing is too small for God. He wants to know about every paper cut and every scrape so that He can pour the balm of His mercy into them. I am reminded of this verse from the Psalms: "My wounds grow foul and fester because of my foolishness" (38:5). My foolishness is this: I do not go to Him to receive His mercy. He wants—as any good parent wants—for us to bring Him everything that hurts. When someone says a harsh word to us, when someone glances at us resentfully and we grow discouraged, when we become frightened, or when we fall into the same sin again, He wants to pour His mercy into it all. All we have to do is turn to Him and receive it. We have to make this choice to receive from Him because, as Mother Teresa explains, He doesn't force Himself in.[8]

---

[8] Mother Teresa, *Come Be My Light*, 260.

The Light of His Eyes

In the Midst of the Mess

It is much easier for us to believe we are loved when we are "being good," but so often our sinfulness makes us hide from God in shame. In such a state, we ask ourselves, "How could God love me when I'm such a mess? How could He love me when I've been such a mess in the past?" I know I've asked these questions many times in my life.

I recall a little comical scene in our monastery chapel that would lead to a deeper understanding that He is there with me, present in the midst of all my messes. Because one of our sisters was missing that evening, I was one place ahead in line to receive my blessing from my superior after Vespers. The sister behind me quietly teased that I was Jacob, stealing my sister's blessing. I turned around and exclaimed, rather loudly, "Just call me Israel!" I surprised myself with my response, especially since we are supposed to be quiet in the chapel. What could I do except shake my head and chuckle at my surprising behavior as I walked away?

Later that night, I had the opportunity to spend several hours in the chapel in quiet prayer. Soon I realized that all I was doing was dwelling on the sins of my childhood. No matter what I did, I could not seem to think of anything else. I was not sitting peacefully with my Father in His love in the present moment; instead, all I could think about was my past. Finally, I cried out to the Father, "Did You love me even then?" He kept prompting me to read from the prophet Hosea, but I did not have my Bible with me in the chapel. Yet His prompting was relentless, so at last I borrowed my sister's Bible and opened to these words: "When *Israel* was a child, I loved him" (Hos. 11:1, emphasis added). Although this is what I read, as I had only just loudly proclaimed to everyone that I should be called "Israel," all I heard in my heart was the Father saying to me, "When Iliana was a child, I loved her." It was as if He had allowed my past to enter the present moment so that there, in that present moment, I could receive His love for me as a child. Even in the midst of all the mess I had made, He loved me.

Restoration

On one of my retreats, I realized that I did not really know what to expect from my time there, so I asked God what He most wanted to address. He responded, "Your beauty." I was so startled that I jumped. During my prayer time on one of the days of that retreat, I was reminded of one of my earliest childhood memories. My dad is a priest (this is normal for parish priests in the Eastern churches, both Catholic and Orthodox). When I was little, I would go with him to the Basilica of the National Shrine of the Immaculate Conception in Washington, DC, and he would celebrate Divine Liturgy in the Byzantine chapel. From the time I was very young, he would bring me with him to the sacristy as he prepared for the Divine Liturgy. I would immediately hide amidst all the vestments that hung there, smelling the incense on them, watching from my little hiding spot as my dad went through his preparations. Those moments constitute perhaps some of the safest, most beautiful memories of my life.

Then, as I remembered those early days, the Father began to show me many things. First, He showed me all the desires that had been present in that little heart of mine. In my simplicity, I longed to know God, I longed to be a saint, and I longed for Heaven. And then God showed me how the devil would go on to take advantage of these desires as I grew older, leading me deeper into self-rejection with every sin that I committed. God showed me how the devil's mockery would leave me bound up and ashamed, afraid to be myself. Then He went back and showed me that same scene all over again, except that this time I could see Him right beside me, and, through His grace, *I could see Him seeing* my beauty. I saw His love for this little, joyful, and ardent child that longed for Heaven. I understood that I was beautiful to Him in that moment. Later, He would take me through all the times in my life that were the most sinful. And even during those times, when I thought myself most worthy of rejection, most unlovable, He still stood there. With that same look of love, He kept speaking to me, "That's not what you're made for," always calling me back to the dignity and the beauty of my Baptism.

That same evening of that retreat, I went to Adoration. I looked everywhere for a place to sit, but the chapel was crowded, and I found none, so I sat on the floor instead. I was not content, because I had a desire to find a "little hiding spot" where I could imagine I was alone with Jesus. The middle of the floor in a crowded room was anything but such a spot. After the readings, the priest instructed us to sit for the homily, so I looked around again. To my relief, I saw a little spot in the corner of the room. I was thrilled, and I sat there in stillness and peace. After the homily, the priest came to the back of the chapel and laid his vestments on the chair next to mine. Without expecting it or even realizing that this is what had happened, I found that I was that small child again, hiding amidst the vestments. I heard the Father say, "You can touch them." I hesitated for a moment, and He said, "I want my little girl back." I was pierced. So much was healed and restored within me. I knew that I had been seen and loved.

This healing would still need to go deeper, but in this moment I truly opened my heart to receive His healing touch.

As I sat there and held the tassels of the vestments in my hand, I was reminded of another moment of grace from the past. I had been sitting on the floor of a church one day, praying after Confession. In my prayer, I suddenly became aware of someone standing next to me. For some reason, I assumed that it was my dad in his long cassock. I leaned on his leg, and as I played with the fringe of his cassock, he placed his hand on my head. I looked up and realized that it was not my dad at all, but Jesus, standing right beside me. I imagined the scene of the hemorrhaging woman, reaching out to touch Jesus' cloak (see Mark 5:25–34). I was taken back to that same scene, resting my head on His legs as I played with the fringe of His robe. Previously, I had always imagined that Jesus was walking away and that I was reaching out toward Him. But now I could see that I did not need to reach out. All I had to do was lean in, because He was right there. He used my dad's priesthood to help me recognize who my true Father was—namely, God Himself.

Several months later, a priest in Confession helped this healing to penetrate more deeply into my soul. I knew even as I sat in that confessional chair that something was being healed and renewed within me. I knew it was a Confession I would not forget. As I bowed my head and closed my eyes to receive absolution, something very unexpected happened: The priest placed the end of his stole in my hand! I accepted it, holding it in my hands as he placed his hand on my head, restoring me to my childhood innocence. I would never be able to explain why the priest did this, but I understood that the Holy Spirit had prompted him to do something rather unusual, something that allowed His little daughter to receive His love in a deeper way—something to restore within her soul all that was broken.

To be known and still to be loved—is this not the cry of every human heart? Then it sees something it has not always seen: It has *always* been known and has *always* been infinitely loved. This truth is transformative. Jesus said to the Jews who believed in Him, "You will know the truth, and the truth will make you free" (John 8:32). Through the power of the Holy Spirit, truth pierces the heart, renews it, and restores it, setting it ablaze with the unquenchable fire of Divine Love.

Within the Flames

In sickness, I lie and gaze at the Sacred Heart.
    The lance has rent His flesh asunder.
    The heavens resound with claps of thunder.
      The veil is torn apart.

In sickness, I enter the Holy of Holies.
    This is where He gives me His Love.
    I do nothing but gaze as a witless dove,
      my weakness revealing His Glories.

In sickness, I am within the Flames.
    He kisses me upon my bed,
    whose sin caused Him to be dead.
      His mercy all things claims.

5

A Child in Need

The Gift of Poverty

On another retreat, as I was meeting with the retreat director, I heard in my heart the words "Willingly I will boast in my weaknesses." Although I knew St. Paul had written this, I did not remember how to find this verse in the Scriptures. I could have asked the retreat director, but before I had a chance, our meeting ended, and he had to run to another appointment. I was not too worried, since I knew God would direct me to this passage in His own way if He desired it for me. Later that morning, I was invited to attend a diaconate ordination, and then I found out that a priest with whom I had corresponded but had never actually met would also be there. After the ordination Mass, with the help of a friend, I at last found him in the large crowd. He was delighted to see me, and, much to my surprise, he said, "I have something for you!" He pulled a little stone from his pocket, inscribed with the words "Willingly I boast of my weaknesses, that the power of Christ may rest upon me" (see 2 Cor. 12:9). He explained that he had found the stone a few weeks earlier on their monastery grounds, and the Holy Spirit told him to write that verse on it for me. "And you see, the other side of the stone looks perfect, but I wrote it on the imperfect side of the stone. He's attracted to your weakness."

The Light of His Eyes

The thought that God would be attracted to my weakness was strange to me. Later I read, "We too must experience poverty if we want to be true carriers of God's love. To be able to proclaim the Good News to the poor we must know what is poverty."[9] I think when I first read these words of Mother Teresa, I assumed she had meant only material poverty. When I would later struggle with sickness, I came to realize that she must also have meant physical poverty. And as time goes on, I see more and more clearly the necessity of recognizing my own spiritual poverty. If I am not "poor in spirit" (Matt. 5:3), how am I to minister to everyone around me who is poor in spirit?

I remember reflecting once on the Beatitudes and asking what it meant to be poor in spirit. I was led to these words: "The Spirit of the Lord is upon me, because he has anointed me to preach good news to the poor. He has sent me to proclaim release to the captives and recovering of sight to the blind, to set at liberty those who are oppressed" (Luke 4:18). Jesus said to those who heard Him read these words in the synagogue, "Today this scripture has been fulfilled in your hearing" (Luke 4:21). I could see my poverty, my spiritual blindness, my bondage to sin, and I could see that Jesus came to heal me and free me. I realized for the first time in my life that, because of this poverty, I was not cursed but *blessed* (see Matt. 5:3). He showed me that it was because of my own poverty that I could and would be tenderhearted to the poor around me. My poverty was a gift, and He was attracted to it.

[9]   Mother Teresa, *Come Be My Light*, 234.

Take My Hand

I once had the opportunity to learn about sacrifices in the context of a class I was taking on the Old Testament. The priest explained that God is immutable—meaning He does not change—and, as such, He is in no need of our sacrifices. He cannot love us more or less because we've made a sacrifice. Then he explained that sacrifice isn't for God: sacrifice is for *us*. It is a lesson in trust—will God still provide for me even if I give Him the best of what I have, even if I give Him *everything?* Then he said, "It is to reach out your empty hand to take hold of His."

I was immediately convicted. I think that a part of my heart was waiting for the day I would wake up and finally be holy. I was waiting for strength, and really waiting to not be weak anymore. But a mindset such as this could only lead to great frustration over every sin I committed. Subconsciously, I was trying by my own efforts to "make the cut," but now, all of a sudden, I could see the truth. I will *always* need Him! I will always be weak. Holiness is not an absence of weakness but a joining of my weakness to Him, allowing Him to transform it into His strength. Even those times I thought I had finally "nailed it," thought that somehow and in some way I hadn't messed up, were simply because I had joined my empty hand to Him, simply taken hold of His hand. It was His strength that had accomplished whatever good I had done. I went through a particular period in which I was deeply frustrated with myself because I thought I was praying poorly, frequently falling asleep and getting distracted. I apologized to Jesus and said, "I'm trying so hard to pray!" He responded, "Don't try. Just be. Be with Me just as you are." Tired, lonely, and poor—that is the place of encounter with God.

The Light of His Eyes

As I pondered this truth, I thought of one of the stories in Scripture of Jesus healing a blind man: "He took the blind man by the hand, and led him out of the village; and when he had spit on his eyes and laid his hands upon him, he asked him, 'Do you see anything?'" (Mark 8:23). If I am going to be led by Jesus to healing, to anointing, to sight, I must take hold of His hand and allow Him to lead me. And my hand needs to be completely empty to have a nice firm grip. I suppose that if a child is clutching a sticky lollipop, she could still hold her dad's hand, but that messy lollipop would certainly complicate matters, would certainly make her grip looser than it might have been. In my insistence on self-reliance, I put up so many walls and barriers, so many sticky lollipops I was so attached to, all of which combined to get in the way of God working through me, making everything so much messier than it needed to be. If I really wanted to be filled with Him, I needed to start by emptying my hands and myself of everything else.

Empty and Trusting

During Matins one morning, as we were preparing to celebrate the feast of the Nativity of the Mother of God, I was struck by this thought: The greatest are born of barren wombs. Think of the patriarch Isaac, the prophet Samuel, John the Baptist, and Mary the Mother of God—all were the fruit of barren wombs. God chooses the weakest, the emptiest, the *most incapable*, to show His greatest glory. It was the barren that bore the most exquisite fruit. God does His greatest work in poverty, "for when I am weak, then I am strong" (2 Cor. 12:10), and "God chose what is foolish in the world to shame the wise" (1 Cor. 1:27).

Several months later, I was on a little retreat, and I arrived very tired. I tried to pray, but I fell asleep, and I proceeded to sleep for more than eleven hours. After breakfast the next day, I tried to pray again, but again I fell asleep. When I awoke, I felt my heart asking pardon of God. You see, I did not yet understand that "he gives to his beloved sleep" (Ps. 127:2). I was still trying to earn my way into His heart. This would require many painful purifications in my soul, but He did not need to tell me about those yet. He simply asked me the most important question of my life, a question He knew I could not yet understand: "Will you consent to remain so poor that all you can do is rest in My arms?" Later, He would add to this question: "Remain as docile and confident as a child. I will do everything in you."

This was the beginning of my walk in confidence and trust. This was the beginning of my understanding of spiritual poverty. And this was *only* the beginning, because I did not yet understand that I had to be empty to be filled with Him. I did not understand that my poverty was actually my richness, because He was filling me with Himself. I did not yet believe or understand that I was His child, that I delighted Him, and that I was the light of His eyes. I did not yet understand, as St. Francis de Sales understood in these words from one of his prayers, that I was being carried in the arms of Divine Love: "God, whose very own you are, will lead you safely through all things; and when you cannot stand it, God will carry you in His arms."

Abiding in Poverty

I remember once telling God that all I desired was to walk with Him in the garden in the cool of the day. Although this desire was genuine, I eventually came to realize that I was not quite ready for it. From my brokenness, I cried out to the Father, "I don't want to *walk* with You in the garden in the cool of the day anymore—I want to be *carried by You* through the garden." Then, in my mind's eye, I saw myself carried by the Father in the garden. I was just a little naked baby in His arms, and He held me so carefully and gently. He stroked my ear with His ear, stroked my cheek with His cheek, kissed me tenderly on the forehead with His lips, and stroked my head with His hand. Then He bent down, placed me in the manger with His Son, and said, "Abide with Me in My poverty." I could smell the dung of the stable, hear the bleating of the sheep, feel the cold of the night on my skin. And yet I rested, because I knew who had laid me there. I rested in the poverty of the manger in perfect peace, because I was Beloved. Then I came across these words: "Blessed are the poor in spirit, for theirs is the kingdom of heaven" (Matt. 5:3). After that, I read:

> Without Him I can do nothing. But even God could do nothing for someone already full. You have to be completely empty to let Him in to do what He will. That's the most beautiful part of God, eh? Being almighty, and yet not forcing Himself on anyone.[10]

In Adoration one night, I realized that I was gazing at the humility of God, who makes Himself into Bread for me to eat. He is a mere crumb on the table of the world. Although He is the King, He does not take the seat of honor at the table, nor does He even take the last place of all. Rather, He makes Himself poorer still; He makes of Himself the table

---

[10] Mother Teresa, *Come Be My Light*, 260.

scraps that can be thrown to the dogs (see Mark 7:28). As I am transformed by this food, I become more like Him: a crumb on the table of the world. This is what God does. He transforms. He takes bread and transforms it into Himself to be consumed — and He takes me and transforms me into Himself to be consumed. The Father cries out, "Yet it was I who taught Ephraim to walk, I took them up in my arms.... I led them with cords of human kindness, with the bands of love. I was to them like those who lift infants to their cheeks. I bent down to them and fed them" (Hos. 11:3–4, NRSVCE).

Just as an infant, I must open my mouth and allow Him to feed me. If I can bring myself to this place of surrender, I can find myself abiding with Him once again in His poverty.

Sadly, there were times in the past that I desired to die and go to Heaven so that I would no longer be able to constantly offend Him. But that is not why God wants me in Heaven. Rather, He wants me in Heaven so that we might participate in our intimate union, our face-to-face communion, for a life rooted in love for all of eternity. He came to earth that I might have life, and life to the full (see John 10:10). He chose to live in my messy brokenness, which is constantly in need of Him. He came so that I could start Heaven here on earth already, living in the love of the Trinity within my soul. St. Alphonsus Liguori explains, "In Heaven, the soul is certain that she loves God, and that he loves her; she sees that the Lord embraces her with infinite love, and that this love shall not be dissolved for all eternity."[11]

[11] Rosemary Ellen Guiley, *The Quotable Saint* (New York: Facts on File, 2002), 121.

The Light of His Eyes

Humanity Decorated by the Seal of Divinity

"Whoever receives one such child in my name receives me; and whoever receives me, receives not me but him who sent me" (Mark 9:37). When I receive a little child, I am receiving the Father Himself. When He said to me, "Abide with Me in My poverty" as He laid me in the manger with Baby Jesus, He said "My poverty." The poverty of the Child of the Incarnation is the poverty of the Father. But, with all the poverty of our humanity, we cannot comprehend what it means for God to become a man. How is it that the Creator of all things becomes one of His creatures, even dying as one of them? During Matins on the Sunday of the Forefathers, a line jumped out at me:

> He who exists from all eternity with the Father and the Spirit now manifests Himself on earth as a newborn Baby. He who wraps the earth in clouds is wrapped in swaddling clothes, lying in a manger of speechless beasts.[12]

As I pondered the mystery that the Father became poor in the Incarnation, one of my sisters read out loud this quote from Isaac the Syrian:

> Today the Bountiful One becomes poor for our sake.... Today we receive a gift for which we did not ask.... This present day threw open the heavenly door to our prayers.... Now the Divine Being took upon

---

[12] "Menaion," Matins, Canon of the Forefathers, Ode Six, Theotokion, trans. from the original Greek by Fr. David Anderson, 2023.

Himself the seal of humanity, in order for humanity to be decorated by the seal of Divinity.[13]

It is not simply that He lived in material poverty, though He certainly did that. Jesus was raised in a poor family, was born into abject poverty, and He lived in exile. His earthly parents could sacrifice only two turtledoves—the offering of the poor—when they came to present Him in the temple. Incredibly, this poverty of the Child of the Incarnation is my poverty too, for He has taken on human nature and so has taken on our poverty. "This poor man cried, and the Lord heard him" (Ps. 34:6). The Father hears the infant Jesus crying in the manger, but notice that He does not remove Him from the manger. He does not respond by placing Him on a rich bed of down. He does not take away our poverty; rather, He enters into it, and He transforms it.

One day I was admiring an icon in which St. Joseph tenderly holds in his hand Baby Jesus' little foot. It struck me again: God became small and dependent. He made Himself small and dependent on us so that we would learn to be small and dependent on Him. Then I read, "Whoever does not receive the kingdom of God like a child shall not enter it.... How hard it will be for those who have riches to enter the kingdom of God" (Mark 10:15, 23). I remembered St. Paul's words: He "emptied himself, taking the form of a servant.... And being found in human form he humbled himself and became obedient unto death" (Phil. 2:7-8). To be Jesus is to be totally empty, totally poor, totally surrendered to the will of the Father, and at the same time to contain within Himself

---

[13] *Catechism of the Ukrainian Catholic Church: Christ—Our Pascha*, 70.

all the fullness of God. Through our Baptism, we are Jesus, and, like Him, using the poor widow with her two coins as our model (Mark 12:44), we are called to give everything that we have so as to receive everything from God. St. Gregory the Theologian said so beautifully, "He who makes rich is made poor; He takes on the poverty of my flesh, that I may gain the riches of His divinity."[14]

You Visited Me

Once, when I was sick in the hospital, I kept hearing these words over and over in my heart: "I was sick, and you visited me." I asked God why He was speaking these words to me. Was I lonely? Did I desire to be visited? Where was this coming from? Then, in a flash, I understood. If the Father desires us to visit and care for the sick (see Matt. 25:36), how much more will He visit and care for me Himself in the midst of my sickness? In a profound moment of grace, I knew that He was present with me in that hospital room. It was so profound that I felt as though all my sufferings were worth that moment of grace.

Only later would I learn that this does not apply simply to physical sickness but to every kind of sickness that we experience. He is present—visiting me, caring for me—in the midst of all my emotional and spiritual sicknesses as well. It is these broken places within me that He visits, that He fills with Himself. He is attracted to my weakness.

---

[14] Gregory the Theologian, *Orations*, Oration 45.

Here with Me

My God, how is it that You're here with me,
    a gaze of pure humility?
I sing to You a song of praise;
    now dwell within me all my days.

My God, how is it that You're here with me,
    the poorest of humanity?
"My God, my all," my soul cries out,
    "I cannot now begin to doubt!"

O Bread of God come down to earth,
    miraculous as virgin birth.
Incarnate God, my Savior, all,
    who rescues me from my own fall,
appears as crumbs, what mystery,
    O God of deep humility!

My eyes behold Your poverty,
    in manger cold, on Calvary,
now comes to me as bread to eat,
    and says, "I now must wash your feet."

The Love that burns within my heart,
    pierced by sword and fiery dart,
must be given all away,
    to the lonely sent my way.

My God, how is it that You're here with me,
  Father, Son, and Spirit Three?
Help me always Yours to be—
  abide within my misery.

What waves of grace renew my soul:
  His Presence here has made me whole.

6

Grace Poured Out in Blood and Water

A Torrent of Grace

I went on a medical mission trip once to Haiti, and on the last night of the trip, I was awake all night because of a torrential downpour. I usually enjoy sleeping on a rainy night, but not this time. I was filled with simultaneous terror and awe at such dramatic rainfall. I had never experienced anything like it before. In the morning, it became evident to me that this had in fact been such a storm as to be a natural disaster. The roads and neighborhoods all around us were flooded, and water had poured in from every side into the shacks that were people's homes. What had, just the day before, been the main road was now a lake—perhaps a series of large lakes would be a more accurate description. As we attempted to drive to the airport through these lakes, I took all of this in. I understood that nobody back home would ever comprehend the scale of the drama that I was witnessing. I asked our guide if he thought our flight would still be able to depart. He looked at me without understanding, and so I clarified that I was concerned our flight would be canceled because of the rain. He burst into laughter and replied in astonishment, "This? This is only a drizzle!"

To recount each aspect of the graces God has poured into my life would be more difficult than catching every single raindrop in a monsoon. Yet what appears to me to be a monsoon of grace is, in the eyes of God, only a drizzle. After even a single grace-filled retreat, I could never be able to explain adequately even a part of what He has done in my soul. I can even imagine the Father laughing (see Ps. 2:4) at how overwhelmed I am by His drizzles of grace. What He has shown me up until now—which I know is only a tiny portion of all that will one day be revealed to me—has been almost more than I could endure because of its lavish beauty. If I saw a true monsoon of His love, I would already be in Heaven, in our eternal face-to-face. He reassures me that, even if I failed to ever explain to anyone how truly lavish He has been, and even if I were the only one to see the wonders He has poured into my soul, these gifts would not have been wasted on me. I alone am worth such a lavish love. And yet He is this lavish in His love with each and every one of us, individually. He does not withhold His grace from anyone. He "sends rain on the just and on the unjust" (Matt. 5: 45). The only question is, will we choose to receive it?

Grace Received as a Baby Sparrow

I was once given the grace of seeing, in prayer, the image of the blood and water pouring out from the side of Christ. As it poured out, I opened my mouth to drink it, and I heard these words: "Drink of Me, and you will never thirst. As you drink, you drink of My deepest love." As you can imagine, this made a deep and lasting impression on me; this was how He began to teach me about receptivity. The next day, I searched the Gospel of John for the passage where Jesus cries out, "If any one thirst, let him come to me and drink" (7:37). When I found it, I saw what I had forgotten: out of His heart would flow streams of "living water" (John 7:38).

Two days later, I was looking forward to visiting the Franciscan Sisters T.O.R. with my community; I had heard that there was an image of the blood and water flowing from His side in their chapel. We prayed Matins before we departed for our visit, and, throughout that liturgy, I was perpetually filled with amazement. We were singing the Canon for the Sunday of the Myrrh-Bearing Women:

> You were crucified in the flesh, O Lord, even though You share the invulnerable nature of the Father. You were pierced in the side, causing blood and water to gush forth for the world.[15] . . . You caused incorruption to pour forth for us from Your side.[16] . . . You were pierced in Your life-creating side, O Christ, and You caused Your most pure blood and precious water to gush forth as an ever-living fountain for the world.[17]

My heart was left reeling. I was accustomed to the Lord confirming the things He was teaching me through various means, such as Scripture, homilies, confessors, superiors, sisters, and other individuals who are attentive to the Holy Spirit. But this time, He was being more than usually obvious. When we walked into the chapel of the Franciscan sisters a

---

[15] "Pentecostarion," Matins, Canon for the Sunday of the Myrrh-Bearing Women, Ode One, Troparion One, trans. from the original Greek by Fr. David Anderson, 2023.

[16] "Pentecostarion," Matins, Canon for the Sunday of the Myrrh-Bearing Women, Ode One, Troparion Three, trans. from the original Greek by Fr. David Anderson, 2023.

[17] "Pentecostarion," Matins, Canon for the Sunday of the Myrrh-Bearing Women, Ode Nine, Troparion Four, trans. from the original Greek by Fr. David Anderson, 2023.

few hours later, my mouth fell open. Behind the altar was a stunning image of the Crucifixion, with blood and water simply gushing from Christ's side, pouring into a *living stream*. I spoke to Jesus for a long time in that chapel. I told Him how thirsty I was for Him. He reminded me of His promise that I would be filled, for "Blessed are those who hunger and thirst for righteousness, for they shall be satisfied" (Matt. 5:6).

Two days later, as I was chanting the Psalms during Matins, I came upon this verse: "Open your mouth wide, and I will fill it" (Ps. 81:10). The Gospel that day was "I am the bread of life; he who comes to me shall not hunger, and he who believes in me shall never thirst" (John 6:35). I saw the words of the Our Father in a new light: "Give us this day our daily bread" (Matt. 6:11). Give us not just food on our tables, but give us liturgy. Give us Your Word to nourish our spirits, for we do "not live by bread alone, but by every word that proceeds from the mouth of God" (Matt. 4:4). Give us Yourself in the Eucharist, this bread that endures (John 6:27)—for the bread of God is that "which comes down from heaven, and gives life to the world" (John 6:33).

That same day, He would bring to my heart the simplest and most delightful image of receptivity: baby sparrows. They are so scrawny and helpless—all they can do is open their mouths to receive. In their total dependence, they eagerly await the nourishment that they can never gain on their own.

I confess that I was once very distracted by a baby bird during Vespers. I looked out the window of the chapel, and I noticed him, waiting for his mother to bring his food. His little mouth was so wide open that I could not even imitate him without my jaw locking. And he never took a break. He waited for what seemed like an endless amount of time, never closing his mouth for a second, always expecting, always hoping, never giving up. The second he swallowed his food, he opened again, and there he waited in trust that more would come. I was utterly mesmerized, and I do not even know how long I stared at this scene. And this is the image that the Father chose to teach me how He wants me to be. I was reminded of His words: "Look at the birds of the air; they neither sow nor reap nor gather into barns, and yet your heavenly Father feeds them" (Matt. 6:26). Well, I was looking, and He certainly caught my attention. I then remembered a passage in Exodus: "The Lord will fight for you, and you have only to be still" (14:14). I suddenly recognized how needless all my anxieties had been. Instead of continuing with all my fretting, I need only to keep still, hold my peace, open my mouth as a baby sparrow, and receive my Savior and my God.

I fell asleep and awoke a few hours later for Matins. As the Gospel was being chanted, my tired mind was suddenly awakened to the words "Fear not; you are of more value than many sparrows" (Luke 12:7). I immediately saw the scrawny and helpless baby sparrow again and heard in my heart, "I am poor and needy; but the Lord takes thought for me" (Ps. 40:17). It is the Lord who cares for me; I cannot care for myself. When I open my mouth to receive, I cannot *do*; I can only *be*. I am loved and cared for, not because of what I do but because of who I am, a beloved child of the Father. I am His helpless little sparrow, receiving not worms but His word of truth into my heart, His life-giving Body into my mouth—He gives me to drink of His own Spirit. He gives me all the nourishment that I need to have life "and have it abundantly" (John 10:10).

I thought He was being obvious before, but that was only the beginning. Over the next few days, at every turn, He spoke of sparrows and of the living waters that gush from His side. He showed me countless times that He was the one who would satisfy my hunger and quench my thirst. It was as if He were pleading with me to recognize my mistaken habit of self-reliance, to learn instead to receive everything from Him, and to remain as a helpless child in His arms.

After hearing the abridged version of this story, you probably think that I responded immediately and well with an open and receptive heart. Unfortunately, I still in fact needed many more painful purifications before I would at last relent from my stubbornness and begin to receive His love. Thank God He did not relent in His pursuit of my heart.

Grace to Give as Oil Spilled

Exactly one year went by after the lesson of the baby bird. Despite my initial exuberance at the revelations of this incidence, I was still very much unaware of how bound up, frightened, and self-reliant I remained. I had not forgotten the baby bird, but I did not know how to apply these lessons to my daily life.

I was sick in bed during Holy Week that year, feeling frustrated that I was missing all the services and all my prayer times. At last, on Holy Saturday, I was well enough to go to the icon corner in my room for some quiet, upright prayer (those of you who are sick or who have been sick for long periods of time know how cherished these upright moments are). But my hands were unsteady, and as I poured oil into my hanging lamp, I accidentally spilled it all over my icon corner. Instead of having the prayer time I so desired, I had to spend the next hour trying to clean up the mess. "What a waste," I thought.

The next day, after all the Paschal services, my spiritual father unexpectedly stopped by. In an attempt to be funny, I said, "I know what Jesus says about the wise virgins who have oil in their lamps, and I know what He says about the unwise virgins who run out of their oil, but what about the ones who spill their oil all over their icon corners?" Instead of laughing, he looked at me seriously and said, "You are the woman who poured her oil over Jesus." My heart was immediately and unexpectedly stirred at his sincere response.

Later, the Lord would show me that, just as the oil poured over Jesus was not a waste, so too our love is poured out but is never wasted. I could see now how often I had been afraid to "waste" my love because I thought it would not be received. Or, worse yet, I feared giving my love to those who didn't "deserve" it. But I was seeing more clearly than ever that I was most called to pour my love out over the seemingly "undeserving," and that my love would never be wasted. I did not need to worry about controlling the outcomes of this pouring out; they were not my concern. All I had to do was to try to unite my outpourings to Him who would use them in any way that He wished. I realized that as I "poured oil" over "the least of these my brethren" (Matt. 25:40), I was in fact pouring it over the wounds of Jesus. This love of mine, freely and unstintingly given, was a consolation to His wounded heart. I had felt so frustrated and inconvenienced by the oil spill because I thought it had taken away my prayer time; it was not until the gift of this further meditation, thanks to my spiritual father, that I realized this oil spill was in fact extremely valuable prayer time.

As this reflection began to permeate and settle into the pores of my heart, my eyes were opened to deeper levels of understanding. The myrrh-bearing women planned to anoint part of Jesus' dead body, but their mission failed. They were sent instead to tell the disciples that Jesus was risen. They were called, in other words, not to anoint part of the dead body of Jesus but instead to anoint the whole and entire living Body of Jesus: the Church. We are, each one of us, called to anoint every member of His Body, from the weakest to the strongest, and the way that we are called to do this is in loving without hesitation or limit. In short, we are called to give what we have received from Him.

Light in the Midst of Darkness

I watch the dam be broken:
water gushes forth
and sparkles,
though the Sun is gone,
and the day
is clothed in night.

The stream soothes the cracks of emotion
within my breast,
coming forth as light—
light in the midst of darkness—
so that, seeing, I may believe
the unbelievable.

My God, You are leaking;
discretion put aside
in the midst of violence,
You reveal to the dying earth
that the Source of Life
is within You.

You give the Source away,
keeping nothing of Yourself
for Yourself;
You show me, and I see
You give me, and I drink
the Life of the world.

7

Brighter Than the Sun

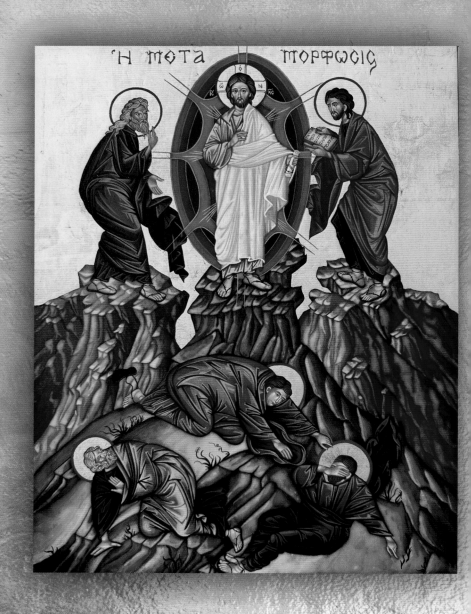

One Step Closer to the Sun

Walking down the road by the monastery one afternoon, I was blinded by the brightness of the sun. As I continued to walk, I realized I was so blinded that I couldn't even see the trees to my left, the fields to my right, or the birds that I heard chirping all around me. I had to keep my head down, and I could only see my two feet walking along the road. Nevertheless, I continued to walk until the time came to turn back. When I rotated, I noticed something else. Now that the sun was behind me, it was no longer blinding me, and I could suddenly see everything around me very clearly. The fields, the trees, and the birds flying around were all illuminated by the brightness of the sun.

It struck me that these two little images are like our lives of prayer. Sometimes, the Lord is acting so much in our lives that we can't seem to see anything at all. We are blinded and overwhelmed by His rays. With our heads down in an instinctive shielding of our senses, we think we are in total darkness—but, in fact, He is all around us. At other times, we also cannot see *Him*, but if we are observant, we can see that He is present because we can see Him in *everything*. We can know that, even though we cannot see Him directly, He is still doing His work in us. Both of these seasons, different as they are, help us to learn to trust Him. He always keeps His promise that He will not leave or forsake us, that He will not leave us orphans, and that He will always be with us (see Deut. 31:6, John 14:18, and Matt. 28:20). Will we continue to take each step to follow Him, even when we can't see what comes next?

An Abyss of Love

I experienced one such season of illuminated blindness during a retreat several years ago. The first part of the retreat was utter bliss. I had never encountered such a torrent of grace, and by the sixth day, I thought I had gained a perfect understanding of His unconditional love and mercy. I thought I would never doubt His love again. This is a cautionary tale to remind me to beware of such overconfidence in my own ability to trust; rather than believing myself capable of such perfection, I should instead cast myself into His mercy.

On the evening of that sixth day, I sat down for one of my holy hours, and as I prayed, I was reminded of a sin I had committed many years before. It was one of those memories that had effectively ceased to exist in my mind long ago. I suspect I had blocked it out because I knew I couldn't handle the pain of looking at it. But suddenly there it was, confronting my soul. I cried out, "I hate this! I hate this memory! I wish it had never happened. I wish I could erase it. My God, forgive me!" As the memory returned, I remembered that I had confessed this sin long ago, but even so, along with the memory came a sea of shame that crashed violently over my soul. I simply could not face it, so I ran.

I went outside and saw that it was about to rain. I didn't care. I hurried to a cemetery at the top of the hill and just sat in the cemetery, alone amongst the gravestones, crying in the rain. After a while, I heard Him ask, "What are you doing here, Eli'jah?" (1 Kings 19:13). I was surprised by my response: "I just want to die! It is all too much. I'm so filled with zeal for You, and yet I'm so broken and weak!" After this cry, I sat upright and was still. The Lord was calling to me. Everything around me was still. The rain began to subside, and the sun started to sink below the horizon. As I looked ahead, I noticed a golden orb throbbing in front of my eyes. "What am I seeing?" I asked. I understood that it was the reflection of the sun in a water droplet on my glasses. I asked again, "What is this that I am seeing?" He said, "It is a reflection of the sun. You can't look at the sun—it's too brilliant. You can only look at its reflection. *So is My love for you.*" Here, in the very depths of my misery, I had encountered an even greater depth of His mercy.

He allowed this memory to resurface because He wanted to purify it through His love. My confessor would tell me the next day that this memory, so abhorrent to me only one day before, would become an icon at which I could gaze, for I would see in it Jesus' call upon my heart. He makes "all things new" (Rev. 21:5). I was blind to the work He was doing in my soul and had felt myself in utter darkness. And yet in reality He was working a miraculous healing within my soul. He introduced me to the abyss of my misery so that He could also reveal to me the infinite and all-encompassing abyss of His love. It was, in fact, a torrent of grace, mercifully veiled in such a way that I could endure it. This is what the Holy Spirit does. He convicts us, rather than condemns us, so that we learn to be contrite of heart. One day, through grace, we will reach that point where we can willingly boast of our weaknesses, for we will understand just how fully they allow us to rejoice in His mercy and believe that His grace is sufficient to heal all of them (see 2 Cor. 12:9).

The Light of His Eyes

His Still, Small Voice

One year, when my community was hosting a summer camp for teen girls, two particular moments stood out for me that, together, led to a private epiphany. First, during one of our morning Divine Liturgies, when our chaplain turned around for the blessing, I was struck by his glowing countenance. I was able to see with my eyes a reflection of how the Father delights to bless His children. And then, later that same day, one of our local seminarians came to give a talk; afterward, he stayed for Vespers. Between the teens, chaperones, and nuns, there were about thirty-four women in the chapel singing, and then there was just this one seminarian. Though he sang quietly, I could hear his deeper tone below all the other voices. It was amazing to me that he could sing so softly and yet still be heard amid so many other voices.

As I thought on these two moments, I wondered to myself: In the chaos of all that clamors for our attention in this world, are we still attentive enough to recognize His delight in blessing us? Sometimes the light of His blessing is a blinding and direct illumination, and sometimes we see it in the faces of His servants around us, but His delight is here. Perhaps, then, we can see Him, but are we attentive enough to listen for His voice through all the other noises, whether they be good or ill? His voice is but a gentle whisper, yet if you listen for it, you can indeed hear it. I am reminded of when the great prophet Elijah heard it:

> And behold, the Lord passed by, and a great and strong wind rent the mountains, and broke in pieces the rocks before the Lord, but the Lord was not in the wind; and after the wind an earthquake, but the Lord was not in

the earthquake; and after the earthquake a fire, but the
Lord was not in the fire; and after the fire *a still small
voice*. And when Eli'jah heard it, he wrapped his face
in his mantle and went out and stood at the entrance
of the cave. (1 Kings 19:11–13, emphasis added)

I think all of us desire and perhaps even expect to hear
God's voice in something powerful—such as in the wind, an
earthquake, or fire—but the reality is that it was something still
and small, almost silent, that Elijah recognized as God's voice.

The Lord helped me learn to recognize His voice within the
silence during my first home visit after entering the monastery.
After being fed by God in the wilderness for many months,
I thought I was devoted to prayer. Alas, when I got home, it
took only a day for me to stop praying. I quickly busied myself
with excessive leisure and left no time for Him. Very soon, I
realized how much I missed the wilderness. I realized that in
the wilderness I was aware of when the Lord was speaking and
of when He was being silent—because I was actually listening.
I learned that, regardless of whether I heard words or not,
both were the sound of His voice. If He said a word, He was
teaching me, and if He was quiet, He was just being with me,
letting His gentle light illumine me with His blessings, and
that *being* was teaching me too.

In our desire to see our magnificent and transfigured Lord
in His glory on Mount Tabor all the time (see Luke 9:28–36),
we miss His calm and hidden presence in the Eucharist—that
unassuming and humble form in which He allows Himself to
be consumed by us. Would that we should indeed avail ourselves of such a gift! For Jesus said to the Samaritan woman
what He in fact says to us: "If you knew the gift of God, and

who it is that is saying to you, 'Give me a drink,' you would have asked him, and he would have given you living water" (John 4:10). Do we know the gift of God that is before us, hidden, yet in our very midst?

At the Tomb

There'd been a Voice—
    now silence.

There'd been answers—
    now so many questions.

The Word lies in a tomb,
    far from His disciples' ears;
    the deafening silence
    amplifies their grief.

Lord,
    why have You abandoned us?

All hope lies dead,
    buried in an inescapable tomb
    built of their own ignorance.

Why search for One
    who lies hidden and mute,
    far from any human capacity to
        grasp?

He promised not to leave,
    but where is He now?
    He is not here.

The joy and sweetness
    His presence had once
    imbued in their hearts,
    now a world away—
    where has their Lover gone?

They do not know:
    His silence is a word—

A word so deafeningly loud
    it can only be heard
    in sheer silence.

A word spoken
    into eternity.

8

Quenching the Thirst of Christ

Transformative Grace in Suffering

One of the ways we can encounter His presence with us in the silence is through periods of darkness and suffering. Several years ago, I suffered from a serious illness that kept me in bed for over a month. This would turn out to be one of the most painful and fruitful purifications of my soul; it would prepare my heart to believe in His love in a previously unknown way. Some blessed souls believe without first seeing, but I'm afraid I was one of the more stubborn learners (see John 20:24–29).

One night, I lay awake in bed, unable to sleep because I was suffering from an incredible thirst. I was utterly parched. I had been very dehydrated during this illness, so I knew I needed to drink, but I was not able to sit up in bed. I tried just to roll over and reach for the water by my bed, but I lacked the strength. *I lay there, gazing at water yet suffering from a terrible thirst.* We do this all the time. We gaze at the waters of life but refuse to drink. Jesus offers Himself for us to drink, and we do not believe. We find it so hard to believe that we are loved.

As I lay there, I said to Jesus, "You are probably trying to teach me something about Your thirst, but I do not know what it is." After this, I drifted into what seemed like a dream. In the dream, I felt the Father come and lift me up, hold me, and lift the water to my lips. I was so desperate for the water that I frantically tried to get it into my mouth. It reminded me of a hungry newborn rooting for a nipple. At last, the water reached my lips, and every time I swallowed, I said, "I receive, I receive, I receive." Then He laid me back down in my bed. Soon after this, I abruptly sat up in bed, and I found that I had the strength to drink of my own accord.

The next day, I lay and pondered these things. I asked Jesus what had happened. He showed me that, just as I was helpless to do anything about my thirst, He is helpless to do anything about *His* thirst. His thirst is only quenched when we receive, and He will never force Himself upon us. He is thirsty for our love. We have to allow Him to lift us up; we have to allow Him to give us to drink; we have to open our mouths to receive.

Jesus is gazing at us from the Cross, simply parched for union with us. He longs to lift us up, to hold us, to give us Himself to drink. He thirsts for communion. *He thirsts for us to need Him.* And yet, despite His longing for us to ask for Him, I had to be as limp as a dishrag before I finally chose to receive everything from Him.

When we need Him, and when we actually acknowledge this need and ask for His help, He can fill us with the infinite—He can fill us with Himself. I heard this cry come from the Cross: "I thirst. I thirst to give you everything. I thirst to give you all of Myself. I thirst for you to open your heart to receive all that I will give. I thirst for your love. Please do not reject my love. I will do everything in you." In this profound moment of grace. I could see my calling to quench His thirst with love—by receiving His love. I began to understand why He had called to me long before, telling me that my vocation was to quench His thirst for souls with love. To give what I have received, namely, His gentle love for me. This is the call of every single soul that He has ever created. The very reason for our existence is love: to dwell within the communion of the love of the Trinity. The more I suffered—and by that I mean the more I was drawn into this love—the more I began to become who He made me to be.

Seeing and Hearing His Thirst

On the last day of my pre-tonsure retreat, my director gave me a final assignment: to go and review all that God had taught me during the retreat. As I sat in the chapel and closed my eyes, trying to think back through my retreat, to pull it all into some semblance of order in my mind, I kept seeing the image of the prodigal son and his father. At first, I dismissed it; I had not prayed about this parable on the retreat, so naturally it ought not be part of my review. But as hard as I tried, I couldn't shake the image of it, so I finally gave up pushing it away and instead asked the Lord what He was trying to teach me. In that moment, two things struck me. I noticed the father gazing at the road, waiting for a glimpse of his son, and I noticed the son turning around to return to his father. I would later realize that this story was the best possible review of my retreat: it summarized everything the Lord was teaching me about His mercy.

For context, I had given my life confession during the retreat. I told the priest everything I had ever done wrong, and in response, he told me that I was "innocent and pure." I was shocked. I realized that somewhere in the back of my mind, in a place I had refused to look, I had never really believed that I had been forgiven for my sins, despite the many and regular confessions I'd made from the time I was a young girl. I felt fairly confident that I was absolved of my little weekly infidelities, but I thought that if any priest really knew everything I had ever done, it would be a different story; who could forgive all of that? And yet here I had revealed every sin I'd ever committed, and instead of condemnation, I found a Father who saw only innocence and purity. I found a Father who ran to wrap me in an eternal embrace, who rejoiced at my coming, who saw my return, who saw only through the eyes of merciful love. I could suddenly see myself as the Father sees me—He doesn't see my sin. All He sees is my return to Him. Even when I was still very far away, He saw me coming, and even from that distance, He was already rejoicing. And then He ran to embrace me. I had always longed to "feel" forgiven, as I was sure the prodigal son had felt forgiven when his father embraced him, but soon I realized that the forgiveness was not in the embrace. No. The forgiveness happened long before that embrace. The forgiveness happened in the instant the father gazed at his returning son. Still far away from him, he nevertheless saw the return of his son, and he thirsted for him.

Jesus is the embodiment of the thirst of the Father for His children. If the Father did not thirst for us, He would have had no need to send us His Son to reconcile us to Himself. When Jesus cries, "I thirst" (John 19:28) from the Cross, He reveals to us how much His Father desires our return to Him. In fact, He gazes down that long road of our lives, utterly parched as He waits to see our return. Mother Teresa wrote to her community, "It is Jesus Himself who alone can tell you, 'I thirst!' Hear your own name being called, and not only one time—but every day."[18] It is so important for us to hear our own name

---

[18] Jacques Gauthier, *I Thirst: Saint Thérèse and Mother Teresa of Calcutta*, trans. Alexandra Plettenberg-Serban (Staten Island, NY: Alba House, 2005), 93.

called, to begin to understand how intimately and personally He desires relationship with me, with you. As much as He calls and shows us His thirst on the Cross, if we do not turn to receive His mercy and love, it has all been one-sided and futile. We have to turn and run to the One who thirsts to give us everything. We have to open our hearts to believe. "Believe that He loves you, that He wants to help you in the struggles you have to undergo. Believe in His love, His *exceeding* love."[19]

---

[19] Aletheia Kane, O.C.D., trans., *Elizabeth of the Trinity: The Complete Works*, vol. 1 (Washington, DC: ICS Publications, 2014), 128.

The Garden of My Heart

In the place where He was crucified
    there was a garden —
    a garden locked,
    a fountain sealed;

then one of the soldiers pierced His side,
    and out of His heart
    flowed rivers of life
    to water His garden enclosed.

"You have ravished my heart!" He cried,
    as He watered His garden bride.

"Let my beloved come to His garden,"
    His dear one replied,
    as she bathed Him with myrrh and nard.

"Now let my fragrance be wafted,
    even to earth's farthest bounds,
    for I have become a living well, a flowing stream."

In the place where He was crucified
    there was a garden —
    and the garden was my heart;
    the spear that pierced His side
    opened the gate of mine.

9

The Father's Delight

A Gaze of Love

There was a brief moment in my life when I came to see the Father's gaze of love more clearly. My dad was celebrating the Divine Liturgy for my community, and I had to go into the sanctuary to light the candles. My dad was sitting on a bench behind the altar, waiting for us to be ready to start. As I left the sanctuary, I turned to bow toward the tabernacle. In a split second, I noticed my dad—whose face was just by the tabernacle—beaming with such love that it could have melted a heart of stone. My spontaneous response was to return a smile of love that was so genuine it likely also could have melted a heart of stone. This created such a visual image for me of our lives of prayer. The Father is always present, always gazing at us with perfect love. I wondered, how often do we notice His gaze, and how do we gaze back at Him? I am reminded of Mother Teresa's words: "I want to love God as and what He is to me—'My Father.'"[20]

Seeing the Gaze

As I have intimated before, the Father has helped me learn more about His love through sickness. Wrestling with all the

---

[20] Mother Teresa, *Come Be My Light*, 211.

ups and downs and questions and pain has led me to a much greater receptivity to His love and to His actions in my life. I remember getting dreadfully discouraged during a period of sickness; once again, I was too ill to even get out of bed and go to my icon corner to pray, so I thought I was not praying well. Just lying there in bed, I began to read one of Fulton Sheen's books, and then I found these words:

> Then there is the cross of sickness which always has a Divine purpose. Our Blessed Lord said: "This sickness is not unto death, but for the glory of God: that the Son of God may be glorified by it" (Jn 11:4). Resignation to this particular kind of cross is one of the very highest forms of prayer. Unfortunately, the sick generally want to be doing something else other than the thing that God wants them to do.... We always make the fatal mistake of thinking that it is what we do that matters, when really what matters is what we let God do to us. God sent the angel to Mary, not to ask her to do something, but to let something be done.[21]

Similarly, Caryll Houselander wrote, "[Mary] was not asked to do anything herself, but to let something be done to her."[22] The Father had told me once before, "I will do everything in you." Simply by accepting this illness, I was already letting God do His work in me. A friend of mine once told me that she wanted to learn to pray better. I responded with an idea

---

[21] Fulton Sheen, *Seven Words of Jesus and Mary: Lessons from Cana and Calvary* (Liguori, MO: Liguori/Triumph, 2001), 28–29, 32.

[22] Houselander, *The Reed of God*, 33.

that I had not considered before and said, "Prayer is just being with God. We don't need to learn how to pray, we need to learn how to *be*." Once we learn to just be with Him, we will already be praying.

As this sickness progressed, I found myself unable to sleep. As I lay in bed, I recalled learning once from a Carmelite that, when she wasn't able to sleep at night because of pain, she would gaze at the Cross in her room, and this would help her. So I turned to the crucifix in my room, and I began to gaze at it. As I gazed, I was reminded of a friend named Joe. I realized that every time I encountered Joe, I felt as though I had encountered the Father's love. Whenever I encountered him, I never doubted that he loved me. I was somewhat saddened by this, and I asked Jesus, "How is it that I can be so certain that Joe loves me, yet I can so easily doubt the love of the Father, who created and sustains me in infinite love?" The answer came immediately and directly: "Because you have not seen His eyes." If I could see the Father's gaze of love, there would be no turning back for me. One glance, and I would encounter eternity. In fact, I would be dead, for He said very clearly to Moses that "man shall not see me and live" (Exod. 33:20).

Had I ever wondered about this before? Why can I not see the face of my Father? Is He hiding? Is He stern or aloof? Why can't His own children see Him? As I asked these questions in my heart, I began to understand that it is for our own sake that He shields us from such a gaze; in our fallen state, we cannot endure such pure love. It is beyond all our understanding, indescribably greater than all the extremes of love that we can recognize with our limited human comprehension. It is a look of love so beyond all perfection that, if we looked upon it, it would literally kill us. When we read about an angel appearing to someone in the Scriptures, most of the time the reaction is the same: the person falls flat on his face with fear. How much greater would that fear be if we could see the Father in all His splendor? There are some things we are not yet prepared to see.

And yet, as I continued to gaze at the crucifix, I wondered. Has He not given us a glimpse of His gaze? Have we not seen a glimpse of His face through the Son? Jesus said to Philip, "He who has seen me has seen the Father" (John 14:9). Then it hit me like a flash of lightning. The more we grow in our face-to-face encounter with Jesus—who took on human nature for our sake—the more confident we become in the Father's love for us. The Father yearns for His children to see His face. Out of love for us, He gave Himself a human face and showed us human eyes—He showed us a glance that we could endure, a glance that has shown us the Father's love. If we would but open our eyes to see Him and open our hearts to believe, we would turn and see Him, and He would heal us (see Matt 13:10–17).

This late-night discourse with Jesus was a very tangible example for me of the reality that I was learning. If I had not gazed at the crucifix that night, I would not have had this particular encounter with the Father's love for me—an encounter that I would not trade for all the wealth in the world. As I continued to struggle through my illness, I found myself clutching my crucifix, and I understood in a way I had never before understood that I was gazing at the Father's love. My heart cried out, "I believe; help my unbelief!" (Mark 9:24).

Paving the Way

I come now to the story I told you in the introduction. If you remember, I was exhausted and frustrated during a little retreat.

I was so tired of always reading about God when instead all I wanted was union with God Himself. Well, that is a great irony, because that is what He desires and what He always has desired for me. Just the brief stories in this book—which relate nothing more than a single drop in a monsoon of grace—should make that fact rather obvious. It is very draining to always strive after God without receiving His love; I really do not recommend it. My prayer for you is that some little story from this book will help you open your heart to receive a love you already have. All of Heaven longs for that moment for you.

And so, in my utter exhaustion, I began this little retreat. My spiritual father had asked me just before, "When was the last time you let the Father delight in you?" Once I stopped to think about it, I couldn't recall a single time! I began to cry out to God in a way I had never cried to Him before. I told Him everything that hurt and everything that I didn't understand. I told Him all of my desires—and there were many—as they kept pouring out of my soul. And while tears poured down my face, I heard His voice piercing through all the confusion and all the pain. He said, "You are the light of My eyes."

That night, I said for the very first time, "God made someone really special when He made me." It was that same night that He revealed to my heart the content of this book. This miracle would have to gestate for nine months before it was ready to be born. Some of the content I did not fully understand; over the next few months, He would give me a deeper understanding through different trials and graces. Although I believed in that moment that I was special and that He loved me, it didn't take anything more than my walking out the doors of retreat and seeing a scowling face to make me fall back into darkness, doubting His love once more.

The Light of His Eyes

Conversion

At last, we come to the heart of the matter. My conversion came in a way I would not have chosen for myself. The Father sent me on a retreat to a priest whose only goal was that I should discover who I really am. He came in the midst of darkness and pain, and he led me to life. But first, I had to die.

I had been immensely excited to go on retreat with this priest. I had heard so many stories about him, and I knew that, among other things, he was able to reveal your own sins to you in confession without you telling him. I thought he was the confirmation I needed to find out I was "okay" with God. But my meetings with him did not go the way I had hoped. He told me I was "malformed," "stubborn," and "the most self-reliant person" he had ever met. He told me that everything I had told him the first day was, in a word, "crap." Finally, I asked him why God would reveal such beautiful things to my heart if I was as messed up as he said I was. He told me that the only way he could explain it was His love.

I cried and cried for days. I couldn't understand what was happening. Was my whole life a lie? I kept crying out to the Father, "I don't understand! I don't understand!" I felt like I couldn't even pray. So, one day, instead of trying to sit and pray, I just went outside and started walking. I walked until I found myself in a little Adoration chapel. Finally, I sat down on the floor, and I read: "Fear not, stand firm, and see the salvation of the Lord, which he will work for you today; for the Egyptians whom you see today, you shall never see again. The Lord will fight for you, and you have only to be still" (Exod. 14:13–14). I had read this passage countless times before; rather than dwelling on it intently for what felt like yet another time, I instead protested, "How can I keep still when all I feel is pain?"

But as I sat there, I was drawn into these particular words: "The Egyptians whom you see today, you shall never see again." I knew I was drawn in, but I did not immediately know why. Then I heard Jesus say, "If you give them to Me, you won't have them anymore." One by one, every pain, every confusion, every person that had wounded me, I placed into His hands. In His steadfast love and faithfulness, He kept His promise. I simply did not have them anymore. All I had to do was let go and let Him do it. They were never mine to have. My wounds belong not to me, but inside His heart:

> Come to me, all who labor and are heavy laden, and I will give you rest. Take my yoke upon you, and learn from me; for I am gentle and lowly in heart, and you will find rest for your souls. For my yoke is easy, and my burden is light. (Matt. 11:28–30)

This passage, a favorite of mine, had suddenly come to life within my soul. His burden is light? Why had it seemed so heavy? In my stubbornness, I wasn't letting Him carry my burdens, and I wasn't letting Him carry me. And, in a matter of seconds, He healed my blindness, and I could see His love.

Light of the World

At last, with the grace of the Holy Spirit, I had opened my heart to believe in His love. It was as if the walls of Jericho had been thrown down (see Josh. 6:1–20). After decades of doubts, I could doubt no longer. If I were not loved, I would not exist. It was not possible that I could be unloved by Him—it was absurd even to think it. Suddenly I was walking around as a blind man who is able to see for the first time. I delighted in all that He had created, the beautiful sights all around me. As I walked, I realized one more question remained; though I now truly knew and accepted that the Father loved me, I asked Him quite abruptly, "Do I have to love *myself?*" He gave me immediate understanding. If I did not love myself, I would fail to love Jesus within me, and I would fail to love the one whom He Himself loves. This came so suddenly and clearly that I stopped dead in my tracks, and I actually exhaled a resounding "Whoa" that made the angels in heaven dance with joy, for "there will be more joy in heaven over one sinner who repents than over ninety-nine righteous persons who need no repentance" (Luke 15:7). I was a delight to my Father, who made me in infinite love. I even found it hard to believe that I had ever doubted! I cried out with the patriarch Jacob, "Surely the LORD is in this place; and I did not know it. . . . How awesome is this place! This is none other than the house of God, and this is the gate of heaven" (Gen. 28:16–17). And I cried out with the Psalmist, "The Lord takes delight in his people" (Ps. 149:4, NABRE). I am the temple of the Holy Spirit, the place where His glory abides (see Ps. 26:8).

My sin had been living a life of fear, fear that I allowed to dominate me because I did not know who I was and I did not believe that I was loved. At last, after much struggle, I repented, and Heaven rejoiced to see my freedom. As I drove home from that retreat and prepared to see my community again, I heard the Father say, "My light is in your eyes. Do not deprive them of My gaze." I am the light of my Father's eyes, and I am called to bring His light to those He sends my way. That is why He made me—and that is why He made you. Jesus says, "*You* are the light of the world. A city set on a hill cannot be hid. Nor do men light a lamp and put it under a bushel, but on a stand, and it gives light to all in the house" (Matt. 5:14–15, emphasis added). Now go and expose the world to the gaze of His unending love—that same gaze with which He is looking at you.

He Waits for Me

In a moment in time, you were conceived;
    I waited for that moment before I created time.

On a winter morning, you were born;
    I waited for the world to see My gaze in yours.

Every day, I transformed bread into Myself,
    and waited for you to come rest in My love.

One day, on the shores of death, I will say:
    I have awaited you for all eternity.

Epilogue

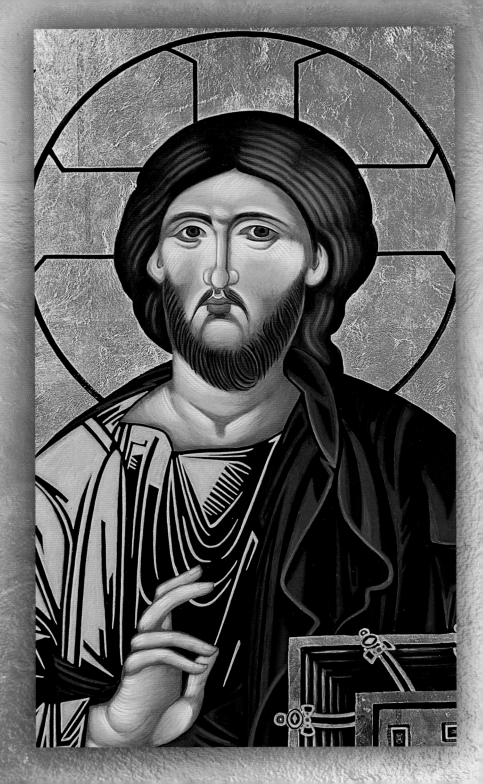

It has been about six years since I wrote most of the contents of this book; I can share with you now that He is still leading me to deeper freedom and a greater knowledge of His love. Daily I must call to mind a word that He spoke to me, or a promise He made in Scripture, and daily I must accept His love for me just as I am — simply because I am His child and made in infinite love. Just as spouses have to repeatedly say "I love you" to each other, strengthening their mutual knowledge of the bond they share, so too do we need daily reminders of the love that the Bridegroom holds for each of us. Healing and conversion take a lifetime. Being transformed by love is not a "one and done," but a lifetime of building that relationship, increasing in love each day until the day we see Him face-to-face.

I remember when I started going to counseling that I received a surprising bit of information; the counselor told me, "Usually, the first few months of counseling are very difficult. I have to spend a lot of time destroying false foundations. You came to me already destroyed." This statement shocked me — first because I had in fact been feeling destroyed, and it was comforting to hear that named by someone else, but also because I had been picturing myself as a demolished building, totally wrecked and useless. When I took these thoughts to prayer, I saw in my mind's eye the pile of useless rubble that I felt was me, and I began to see that all those little pieces could be built into something. Even a destroyed foundation can be rebuilt. As I prayed with this image and felt hope rekindled within my heart, I came across these words in Scripture: "O afflicted one, storm-tossed, and not comforted, behold, I will set your stones in antimony, and *lay your foundations with sapphires*. I will make your pinnacles of agate, your gates of carbuncles, and all your wall of precious stones" (Isa. 54:11–12, emphasis added).

Not only is the Lord rebuilding your foundations, but He is rebuilding you with the most precious gems. Each encounter with Him is a new precious stone in the foundation He is constructing in you. The One who knit you together in your mother's womb and intricately wrought you in the depths (see Ps. 139) is laying your foundations with sapphires, "for the LORD delights in you" (Isa. 62:4).

About the Author

Mother Iliana is a nun of Christ the Bridegroom Monastery, a Byzantine Catholic women's monastery in the Eparchy of Parma, Ohio. She received her bachelor of science in nursing from the Catholic University of America and her master of science in nursing from the University of Pennsylvania. Ten years into her nursing career, as she was working in the neonatal intensive care unit at the Children's Hospital of Philadelphia as a neonatal nurse practitioner, she felt God call her to enter the monastery to become a nurse for souls. She is an iconographer and spiritual mother, and she often delights her sisters in the monastery with her sense of humor and storytelling abilities.

Sophia Institute

Sophia Institute is a nonprofit institution that seeks to nurture the spiritual, moral, and cultural life of souls and to spread the gospel of Christ in conformity with the authentic teachings of the Roman Catholic Church.

Sophia Institute Press fulfills this mission by offering translations, reprints, and new publications that afford readers a rich source of the enduring wisdom of mankind.

Sophia Institute also operates the popular online resource CatholicExchange.com. *Catholic Exchange* provides world news from a Catholic perspective as well as daily devotionals and articles that will help readers to grow in holiness and live a life consistent with the teachings of the Church.

In 2013, Sophia Institute launched Sophia Institute for Teachers to renew and rebuild Catholic culture through service to Catholic education. With the goal of nurturing the spiritual, moral, and cultural life of souls, and an abiding respect for the role and work of teachers, we strive to provide materials and programs that are at once enlightening to the mind and ennobling to the heart; faithful and complete, as well as useful and practical.

Sophia Institute gratefully recognizes the Solidarity Association for preserving and encouraging the growth of our apostolate over the course of many years. Without their generous and timely support, this book would not be in your hands.

www.SophiaInstitute.com
www.CatholicExchange.com
www.SophiaInstituteforTeachers.org

Sophia Institute Press is a registered trademark of Sophia Institute.
Sophia Institute is a tax-exempt institution as defined by the
Internal Revenue Code, Section 501(c)(3). Tax ID 22-2548708.